Panzer Division in action.

"Only Movement Brings Victory"

The Achievements of German Armour

by Brigadier H. B. C. Watkins

"ONLY movement brings victory": the title epitomises the spirit and tactical philosophy of the German armoured troops between 1919 and 1945, coming as it does from an article on the use of armour published in October 1937 in the journal of the National Union of German Officers.

The end of the first World War found the Germans in the embarrassing position of having had their Army reduced to a mere hundred thousand men and so stripped of offensive power as to be little more than a gendarmerie. Paradoxically, it was the very harshness of the terms of the Versailles Treaty that created a situation in which German military thinkers, no longer inhibited by the trappings of large conscript forces, were able to concentrate on two things. They began to rethink the whole concept of warfare on land and to set about training their small regular force as a cadre of high-class professionals round which an expanded Army could be built quickly when the need and opportunity arose.

When considering the origins of German thought on the subject of increased tactical mobility, the starting point is often seen to lie in the recognition of the work of Fuller and Liddell Hart by a handful of forward-looking soldiers. In fact the real seeds are to be found in the writings and stewardship of the new Reichswehr's first Commander-in-Chief—General Hans von Seeckt, who took up his appointment in March 1920.

This dynamic man had recognised the possibilities of infiltration tactics whilst Chief of Staff to von Mackensen in 1915. He it was who now appreciated the golden opportunities for the future which the barren state of the Reichswehr was offering, believing, as he did, in the superiority of small, highly-trained armies over huge conscript forces. He therefore concentrated upon training all his four thousand officers and ninety-six thousand men to be leaders and instructors, in readiness for the great day when Germany would come into her own again.

Recognising the need to keep abreast of technical developments elsewhere, von Seeckt sent his officers to serve with and study other armies and to learn what they could about the use of tanks and aircraft in mobile warfare. Though not a tank man himself, but one who based most of his theories upon the advantageous use of cavalry, it was his broad tactical philosphy that gave the initial impetus to the work of the new generation of armoured disciples.

This philosophy is best expressed in von Seeckt's own words—"In brief, the whole future of warfare appears to me to lie in the employment of mobile armies, relatively small but of high quality and rendered distinctly more effective by the addition of aircraft . . ."[1] Convinced of the importance of surprise and of flexibility in the

[1] Hans von Seeckt "Thoughts of a Soldier", 1928.

L

General Heinz Guderian. His appointment to the Motorized Troops Department as a captain in 1922 marks the first milestone in the history of German armour.

handling of reserves to exploit a weakness or breakthrough, he saw what a vital part good communications and resolute leadership from the forward edge of the battle would have to play in mobile operations.

Though his teaching was more a masterly analysis of the true potential of modern arms as he knew them, rather than any form of military clairvoyance, the fact remains that as we follow the story of German armour over the years, that teaching will be repeatedly vindicated and reflected in all the Army's most striking successes. In passing, it is interesting to find that, as a young officer, Marshal Zhukov sat at the feet of von Seeckt in Germany between 1921 and 1923.

THE DEVELOPMENT OF THE PANZER DIVISION

One of the most fascinating aspects of military history is the influence that personalities have upon an army. The story of German armour is no exception. Indeed it centres very largely round the extraordinary fluctuations, between enthusiastic co-operation and open clash, that characterized the relationship of Adolf Hitler and General Heinz Guderian and, to a lesser extent, of Hitler and his other senior Generals. Not since the days of Frederick the Great had a German head of state so influenced the development of the Army or presumed to exercise such personal control of its operations. Never before in history has a megalomaniac contributed so decisively to the destruction of a magnificent machine for which, in his saner moments, he had provided the main impetus of its creation.

On April 1, 1922, Captain Heinz Guderian, a Jaeger officer and a member of the German General Staff, was appointed to the Motorized Troops Department of the Ministry of Defence in Berlin. This appointment marks the first milestone in our story. Entering into a semi-technical field of employment for the first time, Guderian began to study the work of Fuller, Liddell Hart and Martel. These studies fired his interest in the use of mobile troops for long range strokes against enemy communications and in the concept of grouping mechanized infantry and tanks in armoured divisions. In 1923–4 he worked with Lieutenant Colonel von Brauchitsch (later to become a Field Marshal and C-in-C of the Army) on a series of exercises designed to study the co-operation of motorized troops and aircraft. Clearly, the influence of von Seeckt was at work and the shadow of the Stuka on the wall!

It would be quite wrong to think of Guderian as a lone wolf in his enthusiasm for armour and mobility. A number of others, more senior than he, were also at work. As a result, we find that by 1926 the Ordnance Board had put orders in hand for pilot models of turreted medium and light tanks and that a Captain Pirner had been sent to Kazan in Russia to carry out development work there (the Versailles Treaty forbade tanks for the German Army).

Guderian visited Kazan and got a good deal out of his discussions with Pirner on the subject of tank design. However, despite the progress being made, he and his fellows found themselves in conflict with the more reactionary generals at the top of the Army and it was really not until Hitler came into power that they began to get their own way—though, as we shall see, the battle was by no means won. Indeed Guderian was to encounter continuous opposition and prejudice as late as 1943, when he became Inspector General of Armoured Troops.

In 1928 he was established as an instructor in armoured warfare and began to hold small exercises with all sorts of canvas and metal mock-ups to evolve new tactics with tanks. He has acknowledged the debt he owed to the British at that time and the value to the German Army of the standard British handbook, newly written by Brigadier Charles Broad. This was the famous "Purple Primer", properly known as "Mechanized and Armoured Formations". It was translated into German and issued as a basic training manual. In his memoirs, Liddell Hart remarks how bitter the pill was to swallow, both for him and for his British colleagues, when the Panzer Divisions swept to victory in France in 1940. They employed a tactical policy which these Britons had for long expounded but had seen repeatedly rejected by the higher echelons in Whitehall as various vested interests and bigotries were jealously guarded. The Germans' tactical vision was to bring them a series of striking victories in the war years and to cost the lives of many thousands of Allied soldiers.

By 1929, Guderian had become convinced of the need for the armoured division and successful exercises, using motorized troops to test his ideas, were held. Meanwhile, virtually all pretence being swept away, more development work on armoured projects was going ahead, although the rather thin camouflage of misleading terminology was used. Two years later he joined the staff of General Lutz, the Inspector of Motorized Troops. Here was a kindred spirit with whom he could organize further trials on the Panzer Division concept at Graffenwohr and Juterburg. Despite a good deal of unobjective criticism from the "old and bold", the trials fired the imagination of many of the younger cavalry officers and of no less a person than the great von Hindenburg himself. (It is interesting to recall that this old man had

General Lutz. Guderian became his Chief of Staff in 1931 when he was appointed Inspector of Motorized Troops. "A clever man," wrote Guderian, "with great technical knowledge and brilliant powers of organization."

In 1934 full scale production of the Panzer I began.

said in February 1918 "I do not think that tanks are any use but as these have been made, they might as well be used."[1] One leopard at least was ready to change his spots!)

When the next milestone was reached in 1933, with the assumption of power by Hitler and the appointment of von Fritsch as Commander-in-Chief, the leading lights of the pro-armour faction were ready to press their case to the new management. Unfortunately, the new Chief of Staff, General Beck, did not share his chief's love of tanks but was an entrenched member of the old school. He believed in the tank only as an assault weapon, subservient to the needs of the infantry. Furthermore, he was opposed to the whole idea of armoured divisions. Despite his opposition, the enthusiasm of the Führer led to the establishment of an Armoured Troops Command under Lutz in 1934 with Guderian as Chief of Staff. In this year too, the first 150 Panzer I were built. The German Army had some tanks in service at last! Though built for training purposes, these very light tanks, armed only with machine guns, were to see considerable use on operations, largely because of the delays over the production of Panzer III and IV. Together with some early prototypes of Panzer II they were blooded in 1936, in the Spanish Civil War. Von Thoma, commander of the First Panzer Battalion, took a force of some 600 Germans to fight for General Franco. This first involvement not only gave the new arm a chance to test its tactical theories in battle but also an opportunity to develop the difficult art of working in close co-operation with the Luftwaffe's new Stuka dive bombers. This was a deadly technique that was to have devastating results in the years to come. It was in Spain too that von Thoma worked on Guderian's concept of the offensive use of anti-tank guns. The realization of the rôle that anti-tank weapons must play in attack had a very significant effect upon German armoured tactics. It was a lesson that the Allies grasped far too late—to their cost. Just as the Russians had sent Zhukov to study under von Seeckt, so did they now send other future Marshals, including Koniev and Rokossovsky, to win their spurs on the Communist side.

Ever since Hitler had arrived on the scene, he had interested himself in the field of technical development and had inevitably come into contact with Guderian, whose considerable drive and expertise had caught his imagination. It was largely due to Hitler's support that the years 1934–35 were so productive. The specifications for Panzers II, III and IV were all approved at this time. Indeed 1935 saw Panzer II enter service and the first prototype of Panzer IV being built. All was by no means plain sailing. There were production problems to be overcome—machine tools had to be developed, there were difficulties over the manufacture of armour plate and delays over radios and optics. Guderian was insisting on high quality for these items—and, of course, he was right.

Exercises held in 1935 demonstrated once again the potentialities of the Panzer Division. On October 15 three were established and the Second given to Guderian. Their organization was really an improved version of the British Experimental Mechanized Force of 1927. There

[1] Fuller "Tanks in the Great War".

General Ritter von Thoma. As commander of the First Panzer Battalion he took a force of Germans to fight for General Franco in Spain in 1936.

was a long way to go before the hard hitting formations of the war years were a reality, but a big step forward had been taken.

Even as a divisional commander, Guderian had considerable influence over Army policy, working closely with Lutz. Between 1935 and 1937, whilst the trials of Panzers III and IV were carried out, the new mark of Panzer II, with its improved suspension, and SdKfz 221 (the four-wheeled armoured car) were coming into service. First thoughts were also being given to Tiger. Nevertheless, a running fight continued within the German General Staff over the rôle of the tank in war and the composition and equipment of armoured troops. Although the case for armoured personnel carriers, self-propelled artillery of all types, and tracked supply vehicles was strongly pressed, the opposition was too strong and progress was desperately slow. The Wehrmacht was to pay the price many times over in Russia.

To spread the armoured gospel throughout the Army and industry, a series of important articles were published in technical and professional journals at this time. The most important was the one from which the title of this survey was extracted. It was a challenging piece of work which left no-one in any doubt about the aims of the armoured school of thought. Drawing the attention of the reactionaries to the weakness in protection and firepower of the current range of German tanks in comparison with those of the British and French, it emphasized the great advantages which lay with the side that was either impervious to enemy anti-tank weapons or was able to penetrate and outrange all the enemy's tanks. (The distinction here is significant, as it was not protection but lack of range and hitting power that was to prove such a failing of British tanks until Comet came into service in 1945).

"Only movement brings victory". This dogmatic and fundamental proposition is credited by Guderian to "our adversaries"[1] but it represents one of the cornerstones of his armoured faith. The article put it this way—"Everything is therefore dependent on this: to be able to move faster than has hitherto been done: to keep moving despite the enemy's defensive fire and thus to make it harder for him to build up fresh defensive positions: and finally to carry the attack deep into the enemy's

[1] Guderian "Panzer Leader", p. 40.

Panzer II Ausf.A which started to appear in 1937. The improved suspension, seen here, was first used on the previous model, Ausf.c.

The first Panzer III production model was completed in 1936. The model seen here in a peaceful river setting appeared after World War II had begun.

defences. . . . We believe that by attacking with tanks we can achieve a higher rate of movement than has been hitherto attainable, and—what is perhaps even more important—that we can keep moving once a break-through has been made." Then, putting their cards face upwards: "In an attack that is based on a successful tank action the 'architect of victory' is not the infantry but the tanks themselves, for if the tank attack fails then the whole operation is a failure, whereas if the tanks succeed, then victory follows."[1]

Emphasizing that firepower is the most important of the three basic characteristics of armour, the author stressed the need "for a short period of time, to dominate the enemy's defence in all its depth.", emphasizing the requirement for more panzer divisions to be available in reserve to exploit the initial attack and to achieve the breakthrough. Scorning the time-wasting of pre-liminary bombardments and underlining the attendant risk of thus losing surprise, the article finished with a strong advocacy of the tank as the principal arm, to be used in mass, closing with these words, "For to carry out great decisive operations it is not the mass of the infantry but the mass of the tanks that must be on the spot."[2]

Von Seeckt's teaching on the need for the flexible handling of reserves and for resolute leadership from the front already characterized the exercises being carried out by the armoured troops. When these two vital ingredients of victory are added to the philosophy delineated by the 1937 article and when the work done in Spain with the Stukas by von Thoma is remembered, it is easy to get a feel of what it was that brought such sweeping successes to the Panzer Divisions in Poland and France only two and three years later.

1 Guderian "Panzer Leader", p. 41–43.
2 Guderian "Panzer Leader", p. 46.

INITIATION 1938

1938 marks the next major event in the history of German armour—it was the year of the Anschluss and consequently the first appearance of the Panzer Divisions on the world scene, as they paraded their way through defenceless Austria. By now a Corps Commander, Guderian was put in charge of all armoured troops involved and stage-managed the Army's first major tactical move with its new formations.

The operation was not altogether the success for which Hitler had hoped—there was a high rate of unservice-ability amongst the tanks and the weakness of the repair and supply organization was all too apparent. These weaknesses had been highlighted in the previous year's training but, despite Guderian's warning, nothing had been done to rectify the situation. Nevertheless, his old division, 2nd Panzer, covered 420 miles in 48 hours. SS Panzer Regiment Leibstandarte "Adolf Hitler" under Sepp Dietrich motored 600 miles in the same period. Even today these figures would be something to boast about. Other factors on the credit side were the success of the movement plan, which confirmed Guderian's belief

An early model, Ausf.B, of the Panzer IV which appeared in 1937.

Schwerer Panzerspähwagen *SdKfz 231, the first of the eight-wheeled armoured cars, that came into service in 1938. It was armed with a 2cm gun and a machine-gun.*

that he could move two mechanized formations on the same route, and the general conviction that the tank units were developing along the right lines. Furthermore the psychological effects of this demonstration of Germany's new-found strength on the rest of Europe were profound. The possibility of war had suddenly achieved reality. The Führer had become a dominating figure in European politics, with a consequent boost to his already considerable stature in the Fatherland. The subsequent moves against the Sudetenland and Czechoslavakia were much more polished performances as far as the armour was concerned and served to increase the fears of the bystanders, underlining the threat that the new and highly mechanized Wehrmacht represented.

1938 was by no means a year of purely political progress. The inadequacy of the armament of Panzer III, against which the armoured soldiers had long been railing, was at least recognized by the Ordnance Board and its upgunning to 50mm agreed. (However, in the first instance this was only to introduce the short KwK 39 L/42. Bitter experience in the Desert and in Russia and Hitler's personal intervention were to lead to a further upgunning, using the high velocity L/60, in 1941). Meanwhile work had been going forward in the less glamorous, but by no means less important, field of reconnaissance, resulting in the appearance of the first of the highly effective eight-wheeled armoured cars (SdKfz 231). On the organizational side, Hitler's personal involvement with the growth of the armoured force had resulted in the establishment of a single Headquarters for Mobile Troops with Guderian at its head. Despite Hitler's favours, the tangled web of frustration woven by the senior diehards within the General Staff did much to hamper Guderian's work, since his every action required their endorsement. To belittle him, he was given a mobilization appointment with a reserve corps of infantry formations, although, as we shall see, this was put right in time for him to play a significant part in the campaign against Poland in the following year.

For the motorized infantry, the first half-tracked armoured personnel carriers, for which Guderian had for so long been clamouring, were issued to 1st Panzer Division in 1939, just in time to be used on operations. The term Panzer Grenadier was not to be introduced until 1942, but these early vehicles marked the germ of the concept and the beginning of general recognition within the German Army of the great significance of truly mobile and protected infantry within the Panzer

Hitler taking the salute at a march past in the Ringstrasse, Vienna, after the Anschluss with Austria in 1938. The vehicles are SdKfz 221 armoured cars. These Leichter Panzerspähwagen *mounted a machine-gun only.*

Division. The 1937 article had, incidentally, contained this sentence: "We therefore demand that, in order to exploit our successes, the necessary supporting arms be made as mobile as we are." But it was to be a long hard grind before this ideal was achieved. Indeed, this situation was never reached for the logistic units, and the penalty was a heavy one.

POLAND 1939

We have now reached the point at which the Panzer Divisions were to receive their first blooding in a short, sharp war against a heroic but poorly equipped enemy.

The six Panzer and four Light Divisions which formed

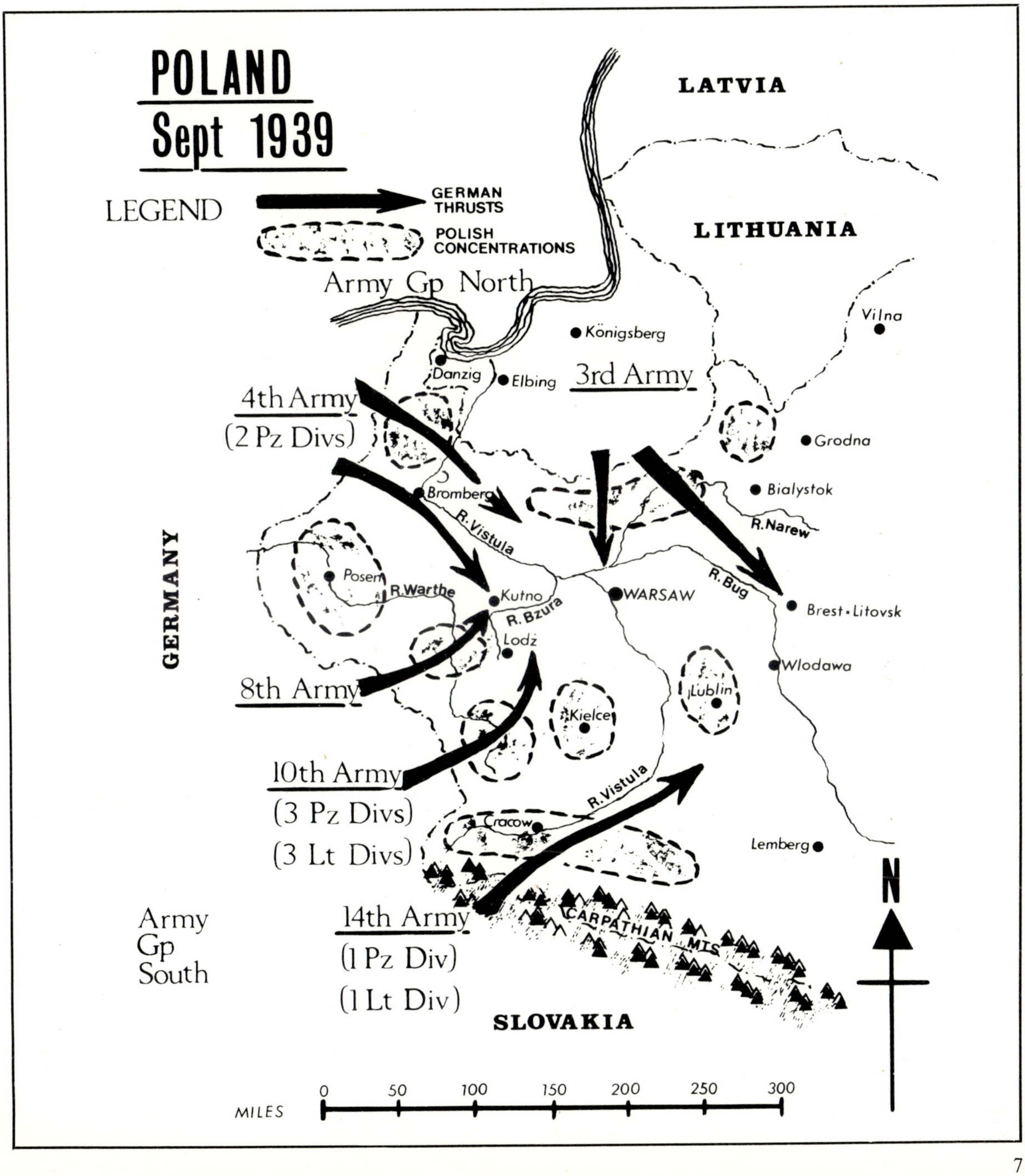

The first half-track Schützenpanzerwagen *(armoured personnel carriers) were issued to troops in 1939. This SdKfz 251* (Mittlerer Schützenpanzerwagen) *is seen during the Russian campaign in 1943.*

POLAND
Sept 1939

LEGEND
GERMAN THRUSTS
POLISH CONCENTRATIONS

LATVIA
LITHUANIA
GERMANY
SLOVAKIA
Army Gp North
4th Army (2 Pz Divs)
3rd Army
8th Army
10th Army (3 Pz Divs) (3 Lt Divs)
14th Army (1 Pz Div) (1 Lt Div)
Army Gp South
Danzig
Elbing
Königsberg
Vilna
Grodna
Bialystok
Bromberg
R. Vistula
R. Narew
R. Bug
Posen
R. Warthe
Kutno
R. Bzura
Lodz
WARSAW
Brest-Litovsk
Wlodawa
Lublin
Kielce
Cracow
Lemberg
CARPATHIAN MTS
N
MILES 0 50 100 150 200 250 300

German infantry taking cover behind a Panzer II of a regimental headquarters (indicated by R on the turret side) on September 25, 1939 during the fighting for Warsaw.

the cutting edge of the German invasion of Poland in September 1939 were still only equipped with Panzer I and II. The Panzer Lehr Battalion, which had been specially incorporated into the order of battle, had the new Panzer III and IV. Both models were equipped with short-barrelled guns and so had indifferent anti-tank performances. However, as the thirteen battalions of Polish tanks were little better than reconnaissance vehicles, the shortcomings of the German machines were, perhaps, of little real significance. Panzer Lehr, a training unit, had been included in Guderian's XIX Corps at his request, as had the Reconnaissance Demonstration Battalion. This arrangement shows how determined he was to snatch every opportunity to gain experience for his armoured troops and to test out the latest equipment and tactical theories under battle conditions. Hitler visited him in Poland and cross-examined him about the performance of the tanks. As a result it was only a matter of days after the end of the campaign that Panzers III and IV were accepted as standard equipment for all tank battalions. Guderian took the opportunity of this visit to hammer home his views on the need for better guns and armour, though he pronounced himself satisfied with the speed of his current vehicles.

The boldness and the degree of control which characterized the German operations represent a complete breakthrough in tactical history. To take an example at regimental level—von Thoma, who commanded a Panzer Regiment at this time, has described the success of his operation to turn the flank of the Jublenka Pass. By making a night march of some fifty miles and by taking a route through thickly wooded and hilly country, he achieved complete surprise. On the larger scale, Guderian's lightning thrusts with XIX Corps, handling two Panzer and two Motorized Divisions as a single entity, and von Runstedt's equally swift encircling movements with his Army Group South, proved conclusively what rich advantages lay in the policy of forward control using first class communications. Both these commanders and also von Manstein, von Runstedt's brilliant Chief of Staff, took command of detailed situations themselves when necessary. Guderian worked from an armoured command vehicle, often from amongst the leading tanks.

THE "PHONEY WAR"

The period of the "phoney war" that followed provided a badly needed break for the Wehrmacht. Despite the scale of the recent victories, the Polish Eagle had left plenty of scars and the Army's equipment was badly knocked about. Although the organization of the Panzer Division had proved a success, that of the Light Divisions, which contained a full Reconnaissance Regiment but only a single tank battalion, had proved to be something of an anomaly. The decision was therefore taken to convert them to Panzer Divisions in time for the French campaign.

In 1935 the original Panzer Divisions had contained two Panzer Regiments, each of two battalions. These battalions had four light companies. By 1940 the Tank Battalion had been reduced to three companies, of which one had been classified as "medium" and equipped with Panzer IV. Because of the low muzzle velocity of Panzer IV's 75mm gun, its rôle was seen as that of a close support tank—a situation that Guderian had long pressed to have put right by upgunning. Meanwhile the infantry content of the division had been changed, so that there were now three battalions in the Motor Rifle Regiment instead of two. As before, the regiment included a motor-cycle battalion but a heavy infantry gun company was now added.

The task of converting the Light Divisions and of re-equipping the Panzer Divisions went slowly because of production troubles and the general state of muddle that seemed to prevail in the OKW. A by-product of this was the acquisition of some 334 Czech 35 and 38(t) tanks with which to fit out the former Light Divisions. In May 1940 nearly 1000 Panzer II and just over 500 Panzer I were still in general use with the existing Panzer Divisions.

Availability of Panzers III and IV was 349 and 278 respectively.

In the event, the Allied tank strength in France was little short of double that of the Germans and much of their equipment was as good or better. The French Char B and Somua S-35 were infinitely better protected than anything that the Germans possessed, as were the British Marks I and II Infantry tanks. However, the Mark I had only a single machine-gun as armament and was both slow and unreliable, being ridiculously underpowered. The Mark II (Matilda) was a different proposition, having a better gun in its 40mm than the German 37mm, to which it was impervious. Sadly for the Allies, only a handful of these stalwarts was available and even these were quickly disposed of at Arras by the 88mm anti-aircraft gun, being used for the first time in the anti-tank rôle. As for the French, their material advantages were lost through lack of an up-to-date tactical concept, lack of communications and so the lack of the ability to react with any flexibility to the enemy threat—defeat in detail was inevitable against tacticians of the class they were about to face. Like the British Infantry tanks, the French machines also lacked speed, a fact that greatly added to their tactical inflexibility. The Infantry tanks apart, the rest of the British contingent contained a high proportion of Mark VIB Light Tanks. These were quite unsuitable for anything but reconnaissance, though a few of the new Cruisers, carrying the same 40mm as Matilda, were also available. It would be wrong to place too much significance upon the British contribution, as it represented a small proportion only of the total Allied tank strength. However, we shall see that the only serious check to the German advance came from a counter-attack in which the bulk of the armour was British.

On April 9, 1940 Germany invaded Denmark and Norway. A Panzer I Ausf.A is seen here on the road to Kolding in Jutland, Denmark, on April 11.

Panzer I in southern Norway, April 1940. Norwegian resistance did not end until June 9.

On February 7, 1940, a war game was played at Koblenz to study a new plan for the French operation which had been prepared by von Manstein. Although the term "Blitzkrieg" had not by then been coined, this was the concept that the plan envisaged. The diehards just could not or would not understand Guderian's proposal for a swift crossing of the Meuse at Sedan by mechanized formations, with a view to achieving the breakthrough at this point. It was described by General Halder (Chief of the General Staff) as "senseless". He and those like him would concede no more than that the Panzer Divisions would establish bridgeheads across the river. Here they would wait for the infantry formations to catch up.

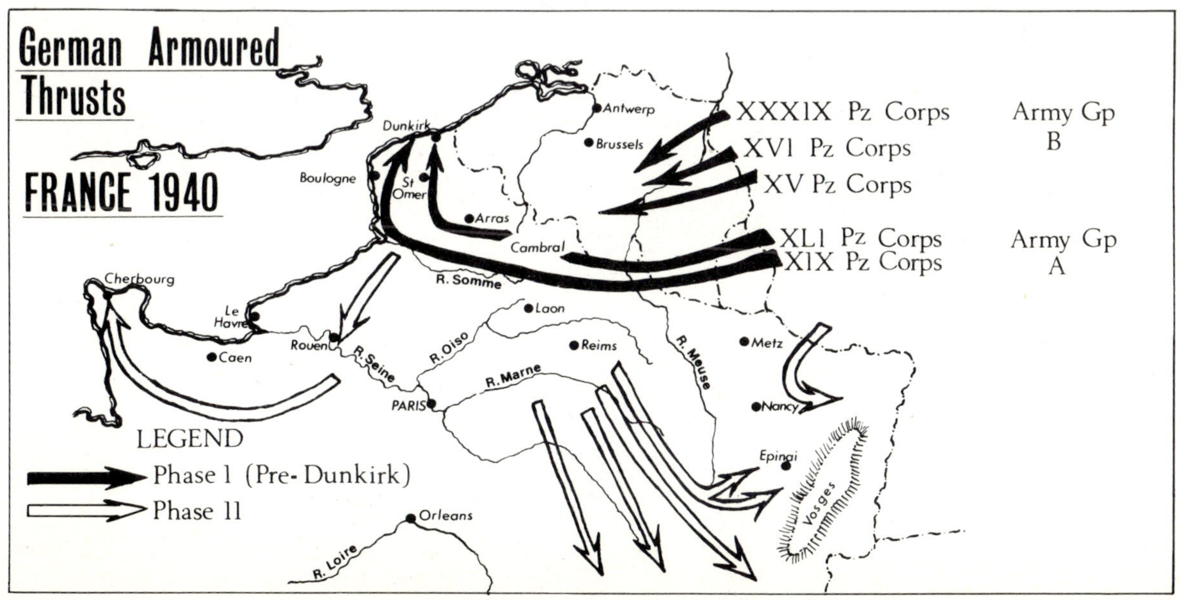

LL

General (later Field-Marshal) Erich von Manstein, who designed the plan of attack that was to sweep the Germans to victory in May 1940. In the opinion of many he was the greatest strategist on any side in World War II.

Seven days later, a similar study was held at General List's 12th Army Headquarters at Mayen. The outcome was the same. Even von Runstedt, with all his experience in Poland behind him, seemed unable to grasp the true potentialities of the armoured formations or the opportunities that really bold action might offer. It seemed that only Hitler, von Manstein and Guderian had any comprehension of the matter.

Despite his depression at the way things were going, Guderian remained convinced that once his divisions had broken through, they must be given the green light, with the Channel coast marking the end of the road. His divisional commanders were solidly behind him and the message was put down to every soldier under his command. In a situation in which no orders were forthcoming, their job was to push on by day and night to their objective.

As in September 1939, the German armoured troops were now ready to go into battle with complete confidence in their leaders, a clear understanding of the task, and a burning sense of purpose and pride in their own ability. It was these abstract factors that were to play so large a part in their victory and provide the drive and energy that were needed to keep up the non-stop pressure their tactical doctrine required.

BLITZKRIEG—FRANCE 1940

At first light on May 10, 1940 the German armies, which included ten Panzer Divisions and the SS Panzer Regiment "Leibstandarte Adolf Hitler", crossed the German frontier. The Campaign in the West had begun.

Panzer II held up by a blown bridge during the advance into Belgium, May 1940.

Guderian was still commanding his XIX Army Corps. Somehow he had kept the Armoured Reconnaissance Demonstration Battalion under command! XIX Corps formed part of Panzergruppe von Kleist for the first phase of the battle, but for the second Guderian was to command a Group of his own. He clashed with von Kleist from the outset. Whilst Guderian husbanded his tanks for the breakout and exploitation, von Kleist wasted many of his in assaults upon strongpoints for which the motorized infantry were far better suited.

Guderian's emphasis on concentration is typified by his pet catch phrase when talking about tactics—"Klotzen, nicht kleckern". This might be vulgarly translated today as "Thump 'em, don't pepper 'em". Again and again in the story of German armour we find a combination of concentration, surprise and the relentless maintenance of momentum at high speed producing the shock effect that is fundamental to success in the armoured battle.

Moving by day and night, Guderian's troops reached Sedan on the Meuse on May 13. 1st Panzer Division lost no time in hurling the 1st Rifle Regiment, under command of Lieutenant Colonel Balck, across the river. No less than 1000 Stukas supported the crossing. We shall hear more about this very gallant soldier who was to lead XLVIII Panzer Corps with such distinction in Russia and later to command Army Group G in the later days of the war in the West. General von Mellenthin, who served for many months as Balck's Chief of Staff, praises the high standard of all arms training which had been reached by 1st Rifle Regiment before the campaign began and which was to become a model for the future. This was something that neither the French nor the British had really begun to grasp—as the next few weeks would show.

There is no room to describe the campaign in detail. As Guderian had foreseen, the Germans swept all before them. Only at Arras did they suffer a solid, if momentary, check. Here a scratch British force of Mark I

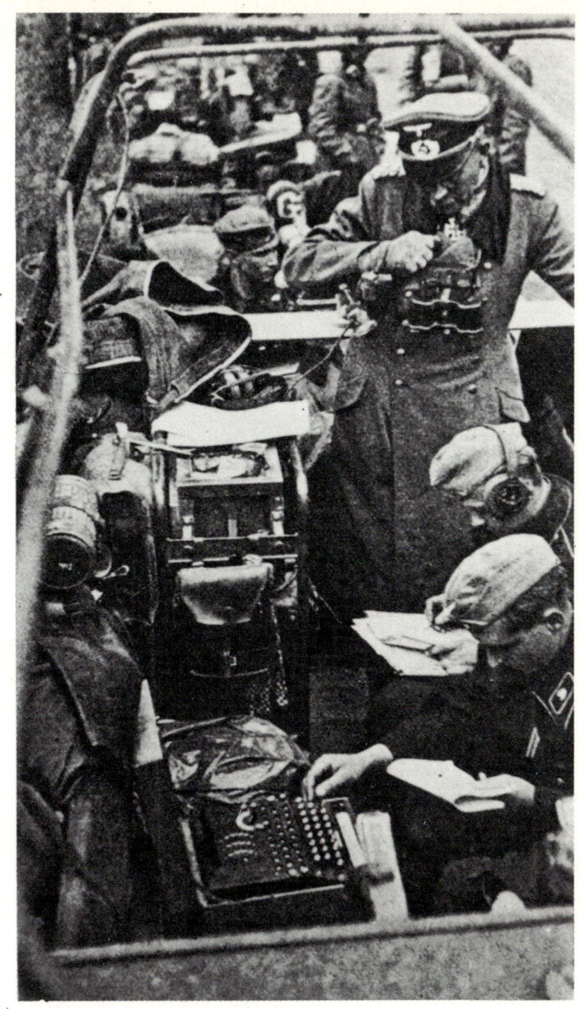

Guderian worked from an armoured command vehicle, often from amongst the leading tanks.

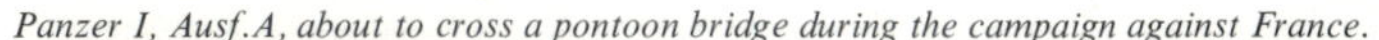

Panzer I, Ausf.A, about to cross a pontoon bridge during the campaign against France.

Leichter Panzerspähwagen *SdKfz 222 mounted a 2cm gun and a machine-gun in the turret which had a hinged wire grille as head cover. The grille opened in two parts, as seen here.*

Schwerer Panzerspähwagen *SdKfz 232 on the way to Paris. This armoured car was the same as the SdKfz 231 except that it had a medium range wireless with a frame aerial over the rear and turret.*

and Matilda tanks from the 4th and 7th Royal Tank Regiments, flanked by some 70 French Somua, hurled themselves at SS Division Totenkopf and the flanks of General Erwin Rommel's 7th Panzer Division. But this gallant operation was lacking in artillery and air support and ground to a halt as Rommel himself took charge of operations to check it, using 88mm anti-aircraft guns in the anti-tank rôle to do so. Only these powerful weapons could pierce the thick armour of Matilda.

The armies swept on to the Channel coast and, in seventeen days and seventeen sleepless nights, the battle was won. The pressure had been kept up from the word "Go" and, not surprisingly, both men and machines were in great need of rest and repair. However, within days, the second phase of the campaign, to capture Paris and to complete the final defeat of the French, was on. It was even more successful than the first. Demonstrating great flexibility, using short verbal orders over the radio and travelling well forward in the spearhead of his Group, Guderian moved so fast that OKW would not believe his staff when they reported that they were on the Swiss frontier and their task completed. During this operation Guderian was visited by Dr Todt, responsible for armament production, to discuss the future tank production programme in the light of recent experience. These liaison visits at the highest level were quite normal and it is noticeable that they invariably had an effect on equipment policy within a very short time.

Despite their prodigious efforts and consequent fatigue, it is clear that the morale of the Panzer troops remained sky-high right up to the end of the campaign. One cannot help feeling that the quality of senior leadership within the fighting formations had a great deal to do with this. Commanders were known by the soldiers who would call out to them and cheer as they came past, reflecting the emphasis that Guderian and others had put upon the establishment of mutual trust between all ranks during training. He obviously had a very warm spot in his heart for the Reconnaissance Demonstration Battalion. On page 130 of "Panzer Leader" he writes: "I paid a short visit to the frontier and had a word with the leaders of the reconnaissance battalion. It was thanks to their tireless efforts that we had had such superb intelligence of the enemy." German recognition of the value of information as a weapon of war was to be a continuing feature of panzer operations.

Describing the administrative measures taken to support the armour in France, von Thoma has told us how each division carried petrol for up to 200 Km and was re-supplied by airdrop (a technique unheard of by the Allies). Within divisional resources there were also nine days rations. Given a rate of advance of some 30 miles a day, including fighting, a Panzer Division needed only about three re-supplies of fuel within a seven day period and was self-sufficient for rations. This meant that the bulk of the available road transport could be devoted to the considerable tonnage of ammunition to be brought up daily. Of course things did not always go smoothly and Guderian describes at least one occasion when 2nd Panzer Division ran out of petrol through sheer inefficiency.

The administrative arrangements for these "blitzkriegs" and the problems of technical support they created were entirely different from those needed for a more protracted campaign. It may well be that many of the adminstrative mistakes made in Russia had their roots in the false lessons learned in France and Poland and in a failure to appreciate that lightning victory in Russia was really so remote a possibility, even for the Wehrmacht, that much longer term administrative support was essential. Whatever the reason, we shall see how great were the difficulties that the armoured troops encountered both in Russia and North Africa through lack of supplies and integral workshop facilities.

Despite glittering success, the German command and control in France was far from satisfactory. As in the past, prejudice and personal animosities were to cloud the issue and to lead to strife between the more senior commanders, particularly over orders to restrain the speed of advance. Interference by Hitler himself, culminating in the famous order to stop outside Dunkirk (thus, ironically, enabling the BEF to escape and Britain to carry on the fight) was a forewarning of a situation in which this fatal wrangling was to continue until the last days of the war, like a virus infection. Dominated by the evil genius of the Führer, it was to bring about a series of costly mistakes against which not even the brilliance of von Manstein was able to prevail. This is not the place to examine this particular aspect of German military history in depth, but it must be recog-

After the fall of France a number of French tanks were taken into German service. This is a Hotchkiss H39 which has been modified by the installation of a wireless set and by a change in the cupola. The Germans designated it PzKpfw 39–H 735(f).

The most numerous of foreign tanks to be used by the Germans was the Czech TNHP which they designated the PzKpfw 38(t). Three of these are seen in the foreground of this mass of 7th Panzer Division vehicles halted during the last stages of the campaign in France, June 1940. The division was commanded by General Erwin Rommel.

nized that it had profound effects upon the fortunes of German armour in the long run.

PREPARATION

The Battle of France over, Hitler began to look once again to the organization of the Army. Infatuated with the question of numbers, he decided to double the Panzer Divisions he could put into the field. This could only be achieved by halving the number of tanks currently on divisional establishments. The sheer folly of so dispersing his armour whilst doubling his overheads infuriated his Generals, but their protests fell on deaf ears. To compound his felony, Hitler also doubled the Motorized Infantry Divisions. The strain on industry was crippling. When he asked the Ordnance Office to raise tank production to 1000 a month, he was told that this was impossible on grounds of cost and lack of industrial manpower.

It was at this time that the incident took place by which he was deceived over the upgunning of Panzer III—the Ordnance Office fitted the L/42 50mm in place of the L/60 high velocity gun that Hitler had ordered. The discovery of this deception in April 1941 created a distrust of the Ordnance staff in Hitler's mind which he never quite lost and must have seriously affected business connected with tank production for the rest of the war.

With the invasion of England in mind, Schnorkel versions of both Panzers III and IV were developed during 1940 as was an amphibious model of Panzer II. Some 50 of these latter were built but they never saw service. However the ingenious Schnorkel models were to be used in some river-crossing operations in Russia and the principle applied to the early models of Tiger Model E. That the Germans were clearly thinking at this

Panzer IV, Ausf.C, at St. Martin de Fresnay, France.

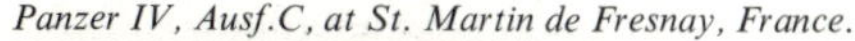

General Erwin Rommel, one of the most famous generals of World War II.

time of battles much further afield is demonstrated by the request generated by the Army for an air-cooled CI engine in a powerful armoured car for desert use. This demand was met in 1943 by the introduction of the SdKfz 234 series—too late for the desert war.

Meanwhile, in Germany, the Army was training hard to absorb the lessons of the past year and to prepare itself for the greatest trial of strength it had ever contemplated. The mind of the Führer was running away with him and 1941 was to mark not only the beginning of war on multiple fronts but also the beginning of the end, stemming as the end did from the folly of Operation Barbarossa—the invasion of Russia. Yet, as we shall see, German armour was to touch the heights before the final crash to annihilation came in 1945.

AFRICA—THE BIRTH OF A LEGEND

Whilst the German Army was training at home and in France, the Italians were taking a severe beating in the Western Desert at the hands of General Wavell. In view of the imminent collapse of Marshal Graziani's forces, two German divisions were selected to go to North Africa under the command of General Rommel to restore the situation. These were 5th Light (later redesignated 21st Panzer) and 15th Panzer Divisions. With the Italian motorized divisions already in the theatre under his command, Rommel was to launch a truly remarkable campaign with his Afrika Korps which not only turned the tables on the British but came within an ace of driving them out of Africa before the tide turned yet again and he was finally driven out of Tunisia himself in 1943. Many British lives and some hundreds of tanks had been lost by that time, but improved British generalship, substantial reinforcements of men and new equipment, and a greatly enhanced Desert Air Force all played their part in the German defeat. Though the scale of the Western Desert battles was small in terms of the vast conflict about to begin in Russia, which involved no less than 145 German divisions and nearly 2500 tanks, the circumstances under which they were fought were such that they provided unrivalled opportunities for the exercise of the principles of armoured warfare which the Germans had established over the years.

There have been many misconceptions over the desert campaign, not the least of which being that the Germans had a considerable advantage over the British in the quality and hitting power of their tanks. As von Mellenthin has pointed out, "the German tanks did not have any advantage in quality and in numbers we were always inferior."[1] To back this statement he gives figures of the relative positions before the "Crusader" battles in November 1941 in which the British fielded 748 tanks mounting 40mm or 37mm high velocity guns against 249 German machines of which 174 were Panzers III and IV, the balance being Panzer II—still carrying the 20mm only. The Germans were supported by 146 very inferior Italian tanks which had only a low velocity 47mm gun. The plain fact is that in the first year of the campaign the Germans completely outshone the British in tank tactics. Von Mellenthin ascribes their success to these factors:—

Superior tactical methods
The quality of their anti-tank weapons
The systematic practice of the principle of co-operation by all arms.

As we consider some of the battles in detail we shall see that, of the first named factor, the facets which deserve most recognition were the German ability to achieve local superiority in tanks at the main point of attack, the skilful handling of their anti-tank guns in both attack and defence and, above all, the quality and professionalism of their leadership, from Rommel himself downwards. Finally, the Germans were past masters in the art of achieving tactical surprise, a fact that was often to prove decisive. Years of thought, hard training and the experience of two victorious campaigns were to pay a heavy dividend. One sovereign advantage the Germans did possess—a fleet of Stuka dive-bombers against which the British were unable to gain more than local air superiority until well on in the campaign and which gave Rommel a superb form of offensive air support against defended localities and columns of armour. By the same token, these aircraft were a powerful defensive weapon when needed.

Every Army has its Achilles heel—the Germans' was administration. We shall see time and again, that the inadequacies of the German system of supply were to bring them to the edge of disaster. Indeed, had the British not been so prolific in their forward stockpiling and then left those stocks intact to fall into German hands, the whole story might have been much shorter. Administrative problems were also to confound the best efforts of the armoured commanders in Russia—Guderian had foreseen all this, but despite the warnings of experience, no-one in the OKW really wanted to know.

The arrival of the Afrika Korps was timed to spread over several months. 5th Light Division arrived in Tripoli in February 1941 whilst 15th Panzer was not due until May. Although Rommel's orders were to wait until his force was assembled before beginning operations, he quickly realized that time was not on his side and that the

[1] Von Mellenthin "Panzer Battles", p. 51.

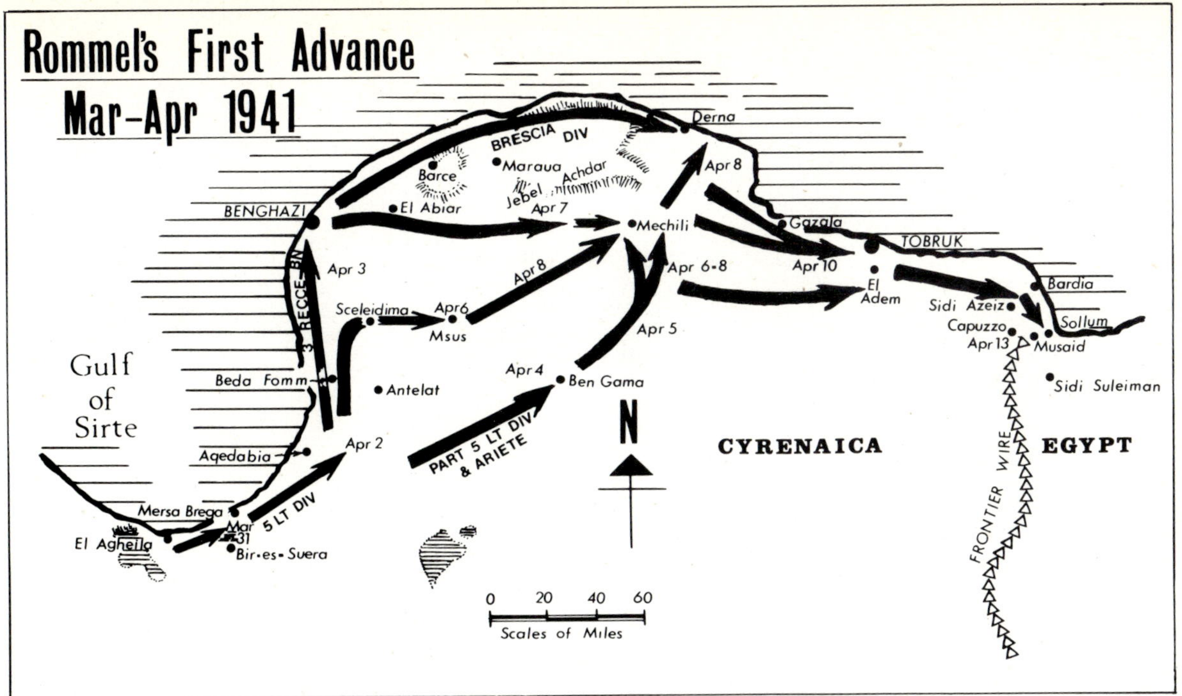

sooner he took control of all the Axis mobile troops in the theatre the better. Against all advice, he determined to get to grips with the British and immediately moved the front some 350 miles to the east, with 5th Light Division in the line, despite their lack of acclimatization. Without further ado he made contact with the British reconnaissance screen at El Agheila on February 24, attacking the Mersa Brega defile on March 31. In his memoirs[1] he describes the deception measures he put in hand, including the use of dummy tanks made of canvas mounted on Volkswagen. It is ironical that just such a ruse was to be used most effectively against him by Montgomery before the Second Battle of Alamein.

The story of Rommel's first dramatic desert victory is well known. Within days he had driven the British before him out of Cyrenaica, was investing the fortress of Tobruk and had troops over the wire in the area of Sollum. More important, he had inflicted heavy casualties on the British in terms of vehicles and stores and had put a number of senior commanders "in the bag". It was Rommel's dynamic leadership that kept his columns moving by day and night at a pace that they would have judged to be beyond them. But the story was repeated at lower levels—opportunities were seized and battlegroups led through tricky situations by the personal example of their commanders. It must be remembered that the German soldiers were fighting in the heat and dust of the desert for the first time, so much credit must also go to them. In June Rommel was to write to his wife[2] reporting a temperature of 107°F with the figure in the turrets of the tanks standing around 160°F. Whilst it was the same for both sides, the British had lived in the desert for long periods and had developed sensible methods of working under the severe conditions it imposed on both men and machines. These skills the Germans had to acquire by bitter experience.

Rommel's operations had inevitably put a great strain on his administration and upon the mechanical state of his vehicles. The sand had begun to cause excessive wear on the engines of the tanks and this, when added to the normal incidence of unserviceability, had brought his force almost to a halt. Reliance upon the repair facilities in Germany and the lack of a sound system of field repair in the forward areas were other contributory factors to his dilemma. Having fought a bitter battle against a mixed force of some 200 Matildas and Cruisers in Wavell's "Battle-axe" operations around Capuzzo and Sidi Omar, in which both sides took heavy casualties, he had almost reached the limit of his resources. These battles were significant for two reasons. Rommel had demonstrated his skill in the handling of his 88mm and high velocity 50mm anti-tank guns, moving them with the tanks and taking a heavy toll of the hitherto almost impervious Matildas. At the same time he had learned that, whatever might be wrong with his opponents' tactical skills, there was nothing lacking in the courage of the troops or the technical skill of the tank crews. One other highly significant thing had occurred during the summer; the Rommel "legend" had been born. This was to give the Axis a psychological advantage

The first of the two Panzer Divisions under Rommel's command (5th Light, later re-designated 21st Panzer) arrived in Tripoli in February 1941.

[1] Liddell Hart "Rommel Papers", p. 103.
[2] Liddell Hart "Rommel Papers", p. 140.

Sandstorm in the Libyan desert, April 1941. A Panzer II silhouetted in the foreground.

that lasted until Montgomery's deliberate counter to it had really taken effect through Rommel's defeat at the battle of Alam Halfa in September 1942. The more one studies the history of warfare the more one realises how significant such abstract factors can become. Rommel's personality and style of fighting made him into something of a hero in the eyes of his opponents and affected the whole character of the desert war—sometimes described as "the last war between gentlemen." Whilst both armies rested and re-equipped, a lull took place from June 1941 until the furious battles of Operation Crusader in November.

"BARBAROSSA"

During the same spring and summer, Hitler's invasion of Yugoslavia and Greece had been taking place, involving a number of Panzer Divisions which were also badly needed for his impending attack on Russia. In the event this fact was to delay the start of Operation Barbarossa, with fatal consequences. It seems hard to credit, but whilst preparations for this attack were in hand, Russian tank experts were being conducted round German industry to study tank production methods! Not that these seem to have been anything to boast about since

Field-Marshal Wilhelm List, German Commander-in-Chief in the Balkans, inspecting tank units in Bulgaria in April 1941. From here the invasion of Greece and the southern thrust against Jugoslavia was launched on April 6, by a force that included four Panzer Divisions.

the figures remained obstinately around 1000 machines a year, to Hitler's great impatience. The Wehrmacht's requirement in July 1941 was to be for nearly 8000 Panzer III for 36 divisions—but by then Barbarossa was on and all the demands of a massive campaign were being felt.

The strain on the German armaments industry was colossal. Up to the time that Panzer III was phased out in 1943, total production for this tank was 5,644, with a peak monthly figure of 213 being achieved in 1942. The chassis continued in service until the end of the war as a carriage for assault and SP guns and nearly fifteen and a half thousand such machines were produced. This was a significant tribute to the soundness of the original design.

Dawn, on Sunday June 22, 1941. After a short preliminary bombardment, tanks of 18th Panzer Division, using Schnorkel equipment designed for Operation Sea

The Wehrmacht advances into Greece.

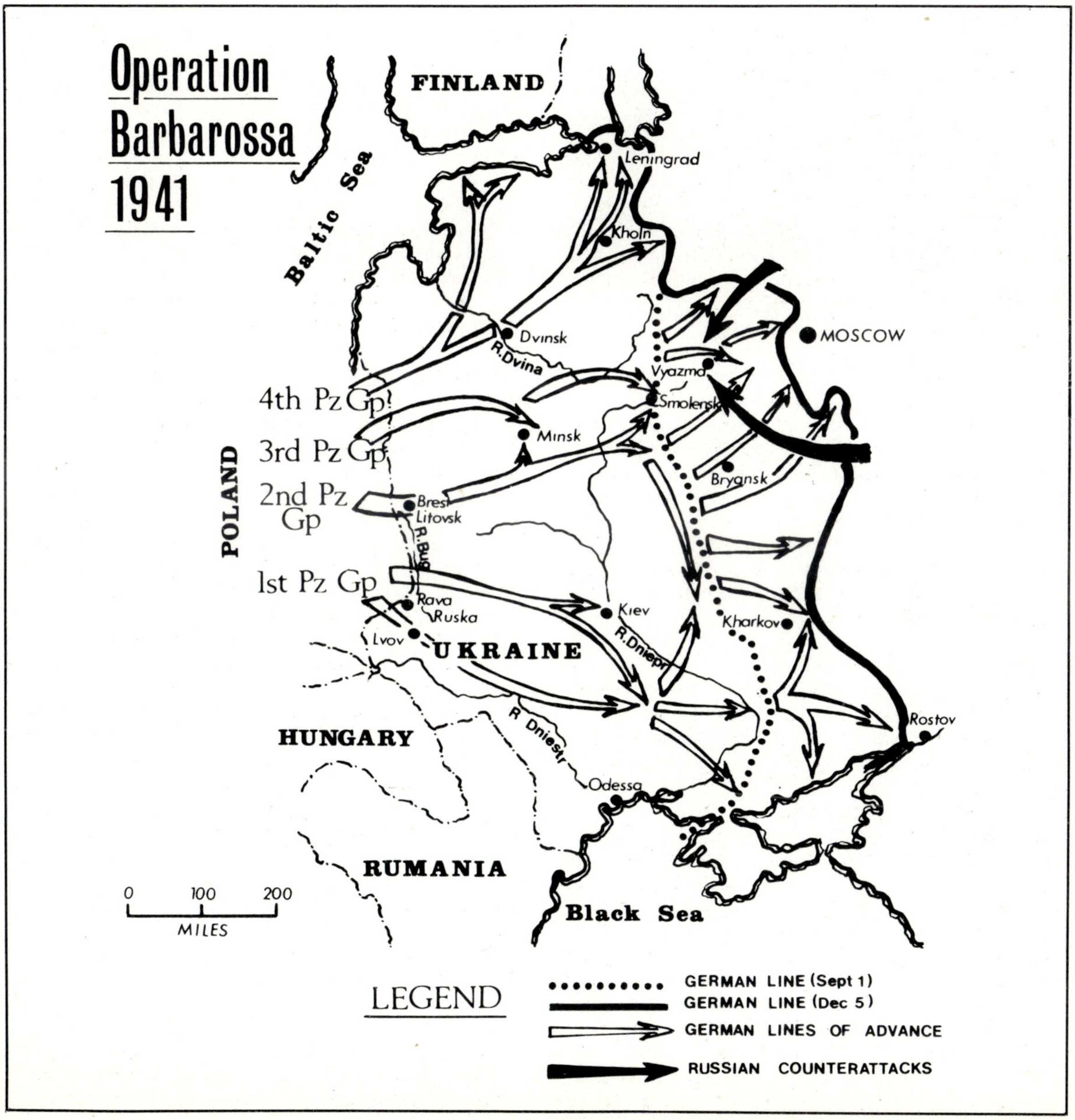

Operation Barbarossa 1941

FINLAND
Leningrad
Baltic Sea
Kholn
Dvinsk
R. Dvina
MOSCOW
Vyazma
Smolensk
4th Pz Gp
Minsk
3rd Pz Gp
Bryansk
POLAND
2nd Pz Gp
Brest Litovsk
R. Bug
1st Pz Gp
Rava Ruska
Kiev
Kharkov
Lvov
UKRAINE
R. Dniepr
R Dniestr
HUNGARY
Rostov
Odessa
RUMANIA
Black Sea
0 100 200
MILES

LEGEND

GERMAN LINE (Sept 1)
GERMAN LINE (Dec 5)
GERMAN LINES OF ADVANCE
RUSSIAN COUNTERATTACKS

Victory parade for the Panzers in Greece. Jugoslavia capitulated on April 17, Greece on April 24, 1941.

For the attack on Soviet Russia Field-Marshal von Bock (second from right) commanded Army Group Centre which included two panzer groups: Panzer Group 2, commanded by General Guderian, and Panzer Group 3, commanded by General Hoth. (B.L.Davis)

Lion, crossed the River Bug at Brest Litovsk. Operation Barbarossa was on.

Two Panzergruppe, led by Generals Hoth and Guderian, formed the spearhead of Army Group Centre (Field Marshal von Bock). The Army's mission was the destruction of the Russian Army located in West Russia "by deep penetration by armoured spearheads" (clearly someone was getting the message in OKW at last!). In this short study we have not the room to examine the story of this complex campaign in detail but only to highlight those aspects which affected the armoured troops.

The advance swept forward through Western Russia. Once again the Germans had proved the value of gaining complete tactical surprise. The broad tactical policy employed was that of a series of encircling movements by the armour with the "squeeze" being applied by the infantry formations. By July 11 the Dnepr had been crossed and substantial casualties inflicted upon the enemy. But the length of the lines of communication soon began to tell. Von Manstein, commanding the LVI Panzer Corps in the drive north towards Leningrad under Field Marshal von Leeb, has told how essential it was for formations to keep moving if they were not to be encircled by the enemy's reserves. He also describes an instance in which his own axis was cut by a single Russian KV1 which took no less than fifty German tanks to shift it, so strong was its armour and so much better was its gun than those of its opponents.

Despite the size of the invasion force (145 divisions and nearly 2,500 tanks, it will be remembered) the Germans were at a numerical and technical disadvantage. The latter was not fully appreciated until July, when the fast, well armoured and hard-hitting T34 was encountered in strength. As in the past, the excellence of the German leadership, their high training standards and, above all, their great tactical flexibility which so often enabled them to gain local numerical superiority at the critical point, went a long way towards making good their deficiencies. In contrast, the Russians were, initially, badly and inexpertly led. The training of their task crews was abysmal. Countless brave men threw away their lives in a welter of utter incompetence. But we shall see that this state of affairs was not to continue indefinitely.

As the battle moved eastwards, the Germans' difficulties began to increase. Fuel was a never-ending problem, the tanks were lacking proper maintenance and there were no workshops in the forward areas which could compete with the casualty rate. Spares were hard to come by and, as in the Western Desert, the dust of high summer was beginning to tear the tank engines to pieces. On August 4, Hitler visited von Bock's headquarters to discuss these matters and also to talk about the future conduct of the campaign. Both Hoth and Guderian were present.

Hitler announced that he had decided to make his main effort against Leningrad before launching the all-out assault on Moscow. This proposal ran so counter to the first principle of German armoured tactical doctrine—Maintenance of the Aim—that it brought a storm of protest from the Generals. No final decision was made. On the technical side, Hitler offered 300 new engines for the whole front but no replacement vehicles: these were needed for the equipment of new formations. Guderian then raised the problems arising from numerical inferiority. Hitler acknowledged that he had failed to give proper consideration to Guderian's prophecies of the mid-thirties and that had he done so he would never have embarked upon the campaign. However, despite these utterances, he was to disregard his Generals' views and on August 26 he produced orders for yet another disastrous diversion, giving priority to the seizure of the Crimea and switching valuable armoured effort to the south for this purpose.

So the weeks ticked by. Pushing slowly eastwards, Army Group Centre captured Kiev on September 20, taking more than 30,000 prisoners in the process. But then the autumn rains turned the dusty roads to quagmires. The German Army's progress dropped to a snail's pace. Resupply had often to be by air. Despite incessant demands from the fighting formations it was abundantly clear that winter would be upon them before any warm clothing, special equipment, or even anti-freeze for the vehicles was available. The price paid for this monstrous piece of maladminstration was terribly heavy. Since both the Luftwaffe and Waffen SS were well prepared for a winter campaign, it became abundantly clear that the blame lay with OKH. One can only assume that they had counted upon total victory before the winter set in and had failed to appreciate the effects of the delays which were the inevitable consequence of Hitler's constant meddling with the conduct of the war.

The impact of the Russian T34 was now being felt and was affecting morale. Guderian demanded that a special commission should visit the front to examine the

The Panzer Divisions advance into Russia, June 1941.

German motorized columns crowding the route into Russia.

Panzer II crossing a repaired bridge in Russia in the first weeks of Operation Barbarossa. The Germans had over 1,000 Panzer IIs when the Russian campaign began.

problems of tank warfare on the spot. The commission arrived in November and, as a result of its findings, two decisions were made. The first was to press on with the development of the 60-ton Tiger, now well advanced, and the second to design a lighter and faster tank of between 35 and 45 tons to be called Panther. The design was put to Hitler on January 23, 1942. This shows that the Germans knew how to cut corners when the need arose. Even more remarkable was the fact that the first production model was to appear in November of the same year. Despite many teething troubles, this was very competitive timing indeed by a tank building industry that was already bowed down under the strain of equipping new divisions, up-armouring and up-gunning existing models, and creating numerous SP variants. Whilst much of this work had to be done under the weight of Allied bombing, work was gradually moved to safer areas in Austria so that it could gain some degree of immunity. Later, the production of both Panther and Tiger B was to owe much to the use of slave labour in the Krupp and Daimler-Benz factories.

The autumn quagmires turned to concrete under the hammer blows of the November frosts. Whole formations were "frozen in" overnight. The suffering of the soldiers and the nightmares of resupply drove commanders to despair. Once again air supply was often the only possible course, with all the restrictions and difficulties this involved under such conditions. Whilst much of the transport of the infantry formations was still horse-drawn, the Panzer Divisions too lacked suitable cross-country logistic vehicles, despite the pleas of the pre-war years.

By the time that Army Group Centre had finally pushed its way to the outskirts of Moscow, Panzergruppe Guderian, now renamed 2nd Panzer Army, was down to about 400 tanks. The cold was so intense that vehicles had to be started up every four hours and their transmission operated so that the strain on the metal of the transmission, made brittle by the cold, was eased. With oil in the sump like tar and the plates of vehicle batteries buckling, it is easy to realise how great that strain had become and to understand how breaks in final drives were occurring. The courage of the German soldiers at this time was unparalleled. By concentrating their battlegroups in villages, they gained some shelter from the elements and were able to sally out to attack Russian formations operating against them. To anyone who has fought under the conditions of even a severe European winter, the fact that the Germans managed to keep their tanks running at all in Russia and to keep up their offensive spirit is a source of wonder.

Between June 22 and November 30, 1941 the German Army lost 743,000 men—some 23 per cent of its strength. Thanks, very largely, to Hitler's interference, it had reached the limits of its human and technical resources. It was, of course, obvious that the time had come to call a halt and to make a tactical withdrawal, so that both men and machines could be refurbished and the necess-

Tanks of General Hoth's Panzer Group 3 entered Minsk, the capital of White Russia, on June 26, 1941—four days after the campaign started. On the left, a Panzer IV.

Panzer III crossing an anti-tank ditch in the Stalin Line, which was a permanent fortification of concrete bunkers on the old Russian frontier before the annexation of the Baltic states and the eastern part of Poland.

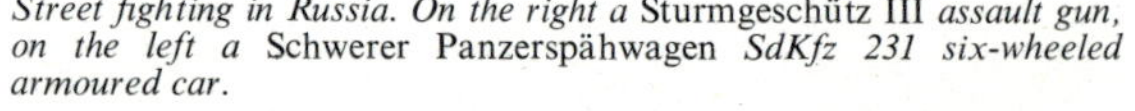

Street fighting in Russia. On the right a Sturmgeschütz III *assault gun, on the left a* Schwerer Panzerspähwagen *SdKfz 231 six-wheeled armoured car.*

ary preparations made to renew the attack in the better weather of the coming spring. But this was not to be. Hitler took personal command of the Army on December 19, 1941 and ordered a complete standfast. The merits and demerits of this decision have been argued elsewhere, sufficient be it to record that no less than 35 divisional commanders were relieved of their posts for protesting against this order, whilst Guderian, who had a blazing row with Hitler on December 20, was also removed on the 26th. Into the limbo he went, until his dramatic recall in February 1943. Hitler had gained a moral ascendancy over the Wehrmacht but it had cost him the flower of its field commanders.

SIDI REZEGH TO GAZALA

Far away in North Africa, Rommel and his British opponents had entered into a fresh trial of strength. Nearly three times as many British tanks as German were poised in early November to begin Operation Crusader—designed to relieve the beleaguered fortress of Tobruk. At the same time, Rommel was preparing to assault the perimeter in an attempt to capture the port. His command had now acquired the title of Panzergruppe Afrika and was soon to be elevated to the status of a Panzerarmee.

On November 18, 1941 five British and six Axis divisions clashed in the general area south and south-east of Tobruk and around the airfield of Sidi Rezegh in particular. The British superiority in armour was substantial (750 tanks to 400) but they fell once again into the error of dispersing into groups of about 150 tanks each. These were attacked by the Germans in turn and, within a matter of hours, the imbalance had been redressed. As before, it was the 50mm and 88's that won the day, rather than the German tanks. Indeed, on November 23, General Cruewell, commanding the Afrika Korps, was sufficiently rash to copy the British tactic of the gallant charge up to the cannon's mouth, in an attack on the 5th South African Brigade. He lost 70 tanks out of 150 and the bulk of his motorised infantry.

Rommel in his "natural habitat"—the Desert—discussing operations with his staff. On the side of his command vehicle is the famous sign of the Afrika Korps, later elevated to the status of a Panzerarmee.

The battle swung to and fro, both sides suffering heavy losses. Ignoring Cruewell's advice to clean up the tattered remnants of the defenders of Sidi Rezegh, Rommel swept off at the head of 21st Panzer Division towards Halfaya on the 24th in the hope of making a fresh breakthrough. But he ran out of the cover of his close air support and, once again, ran out of fuel; despite the considerable stocks he could have taken for the asking from the British dumps he had over-run.

Meanwhile, back in the Tobruk area, the New Zealanders, supported by the tanks of 1st Army Tank Brigade, had fought a brilliant night action at Belhammed and won a striking success at Ed Duda. As a result, the corridor to Tobruk was opened. On the 27th a sharp action at Bir el Chleta caused heavy casualties to both sides and nearly led to the loss of 15th Panzer Division. However, the British missed their chance and the division slipped through a gap to escape. Bad coordination and overdispersion had cost the British the day. Rommel's sweep forward to the Sollum area had thrown the Eighth Army into considerable confusion. Cunningham, the Army Commander, was all for a

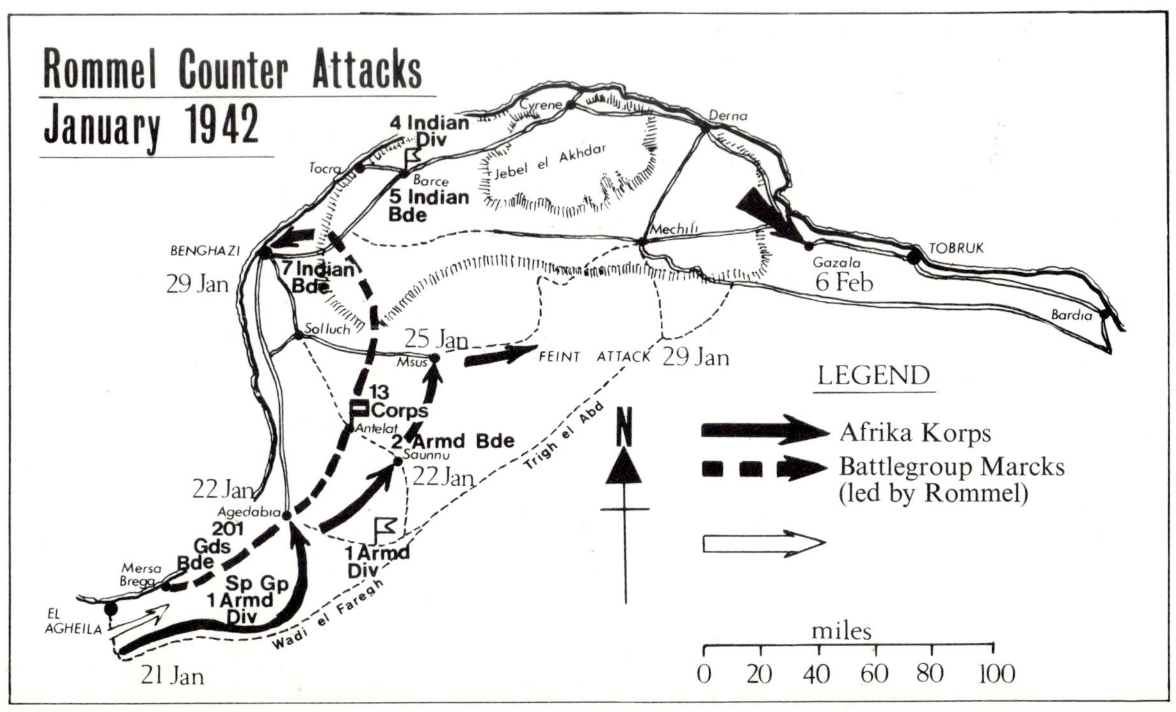

further withdrawal in order to consolidate his position. However, General Auchinleck, the C-in-C, stepped in to order the continuation of the offensive, replacing Cunningham with Ritchie. The result was to counter the shock effect of Rommel's move. By the time the RAF had struck him a series of resounding blows and inflicted serious loss upon his tanks, Rommel realised that only one course remained open to him—to withdraw to the safety of El Agheila and pull his battered force together.

After a brilliant withdrawal, he rallied the remnants of his Panzergruppe and set about the urgent business of re-equipment and reorganization. Some forty new tanks and a further four panzer companies arrived from Germany. Clearly, he was faring a good deal better for replacements than his fellows in Russia! Almost more valuable to him than the tanks, however, was the arrival of Luftflotte 2, which was to give him much needed air support in the battles to come.

Rommel decided that his best chance of success lay in obtaining complete tactical surprise. The Eighth Army had followed up his withdrawal and was holding nearly up to Mersa Brega with a force that consisted very largely of the untried 1st Armoured Division. Using a variant of his old ruse, Rommel put canvas covers over the tanks to disguise them and mustered his troops in complete secrecy. Not even the Italians knew what he was about. Then, on January 21, 1942, he attacked. Sweeping all before him, as before, he captured 96 tanks, 38 guns and 190 vehicles in the fight for Benghazi. Pressing on by day and night he threw the British right back to a hastily prepared defensive position at Gazala, which was reached on February 6. Cyrenaica was back in his hands but his troops and his equipment were at the end of their tether. There was nothing for it but to accept another pause until the momentous Gazala battles of May 1942—an encounter that has been described by von Mellenthin as "one of the greatest achievements in German annals."[1]

1942—A YEAR OF TECHNICAL CHANGE

On the technical side, 1942 was to prove a year of considerable change. Both the Germans and the Allies were to increase the quality of their tanks and, in particular, their hitting power.

At an important conference on January 23, during which he was shown the M.A.N. design for Panther, Hitler discussed the impressive anti-tank performance of the new hollow charge artillery ammunition. The tank experts were hard pressed to persuade him that the day of the tank was not drawing to a close. However, his proposals to concentrate more upon the production of self-propelled artillery than tanks were finally disposed of and he ordered that tank production should rise to 600 machines a month.

The Führer's mind was always seeking for some new and fantastic breakthrough in the weapons field. So it is not surprising that in March we find him giving orders to Krupps and Dr Porsche to design a tank of 100 tons, the prototype to be available in spring 1943. Later in the year we find that a firm of engineers, Grote and Hacker, were ordered to put an even more fantastic design in hand—this time for a 1,000 tonner!

April saw the appearance of the Porsche and Henschel Tigers, for which Speer was able to forecast production, by October, of 60 Porsche and 25 Henschel machines, with a further 135 in all by the following March. At about this time the upgunned Panzer IV F2 was just arriving in North Africa, as were a number of Russian 7·62cm PaK 36(r) mounted on the Czech 38(t) chassis—known as Marder. Both models represented a substantial augmentation to the Germans' anti-tank resources. This was just as well for Rommel, as the new British 57mm (6-pdr.) anti-tank guns were being delivered to the Eighth Army, as were their first Grant tanks, mounting a 75mm gun in the hull sponson.

In May, Hitler approved the Panther design and an intensive drive to get it into mass production began. Simultaneously production of assault guns and Panzer III was stepped up. Hardly had these orders been given than a new programme to uparmour the front of Panzer IV and all assault guns to 80mm was put in hand, whilst investigations into the uparmouring of both Tiger and Panther were also begun. When one recalls all the other design studies and conversions that were going on at this time in the SP artillery field, the mind boggles at the problems facing the vehicle industry and the Ordnance Office. The general effect that this over-complication had on the provision of spares was soon to make itself felt in Russia. Nevertheless, the achievements of the design and production teams were prodigious and were certainly never rivalled in scale by the Allies (although the less complicated pattern of production followed by the Americans and British certainly had many significant advantages when it came to the business of the repair and replacement of casualties).

Despite the fact that Panzer III was fast outrunning its usefulness on the battlefield, Hitler ordered its upgunning to the 75mm L/24 in August. In the same month the firm production order for Tiger went in. By this time, when, as we shall see later, Rommel was about to fight the battle of Alam Halfa, Panzerarmee Afrika had 27 Panzer IV F2. Even this small number was to make a considerable impact on the British tank crews, as they far outgunned even the new Grants.

The first Tigers went into action outside Leningrad in September. Once more the Führer's meddling had forced the Army into a course which was against all the best advice. The wet going in a forested area was entirely unsuitable for these large and cumbersome machines and the Russians were able to destroy them at will. Tiger production went ahead despite this disaster and a total of 1,350 Tigers was produced by August 1944. Slow and heavy it may have been, but the Tiger was a formidable machine to encounter and could stand tremendous punishment on its thick frontal armour. Its 88mm gun enabled it to engage all enemy tanks at very long ranges with devastating effect.

When the first production model of Panther came out in November it gave considerable mechanical trouble. However, this excellent tank was sorted out by the end of 1943 and proved to be a winner. Its KwK 75mm L/70 had tremendous hitting power, whilst its steeply sloping front glacis made it very difficult to attack effectively from head-on. Nearly 5,000 Panthers were made in all.

During June, Hitler had given verbal orders to his friend Dr Porsche to go ahead with his concept of the 100 tonner—now known as Maus, with a design weight of some 140 tons. In December he demanded that the pilot model should be ready by the summer of 1943

[1] Von Mellenthin "Panzer Battles", p. 90.

Prototype of Porsche's mammoth Mouse, undergoing trials with a 55-ton weight on the superstructure to simulate the turret. Maus *was Porsche's 185 ton answer to Hitler's demand for a super-heavy tank.*

The uparmoured Panzer IV Ausf.G had the long L/43 75mm gun, which was introduced in the previous, F2, model. In the end the Panzer IV turned out to be the most numerous German tank—the "workhorse" of the German armoured forces.

and that a production figure of five machines a month should be set. This figure was raised to ten in January. One gets the feeling that he was completely carried away by the sense of power that this endless tinkering with the equipment programme gave him. In the same month, despite all the orders given in 1942 about numbers and upgunning, production of Panzer III was discontinued, although the chassis was still to be used extensively for assault and SP guns. In contrast, the Panzer IV, with its L/48 75mm gun had become the principal tank of the German Army and a formidable feature of the battlefield. No less than 9,000 Panzer IV saw active service.

TRIUMPH AND TRAGEDY IN RUSSIA, 1942

The Russian counter-offensive in the Moscow area died away at the end of December 1941, largely because of the Germans' determined stand on Hitler's orders and their ability to concentrate their dwindling tank strength against the numerous but ill-co-ordinated attacks of the badly trained Russian armoured formations. They owed much too to their skilled use of their tanks and anti-tank weapons, often in reverse slope positions, from which they massacred the enemy at short ranges and so off-set the advantage he held with his T34 and KV1. From January 1942 until the middle of May, the Soviet effort was concentrated on an all-out effort to recapture the important industrial centres of the Donetz Basin. Despite the use of over 1,000 tanks in many of their successive assaults, they were utterly defeated by their highly skilled opponents—not because the Germans were better equipped, for, as we know, they were not, but because the Russians had not by then begun to grasp the first principles of tank warfare and were convinced that sheer weight of metal must prevail.

The Henschel Tiger—TigerI, Ausf.H later Ausf.E—made its appearance in April 1942. This tank, with turret reversed, is negotiating a muddy slope.

Panzer III was upgunned, as was Panzer IV. Upgunning of Panzer III to the L/60 5cm KwK 30 began in the course of the Ausführung (Model) J production run. The next version, Ausf.L, seen here in France in December 1942, was externally almost identical to its predecessor. The series terminated with Ausf.N, armed with the short KwK L/24 75mm gun, the previous main armament of the Panzer IV.

The Panther had initial mechanical difficulties, but when these were corrected it proved itself to be one of the most formidable tanks in the business.

German resistance to the Russian counter-offensive at the end of 1941 owed much of its success to the skilled use of tank destroyers, like this Sturmgeschütz III, *in reverse slope positions.*

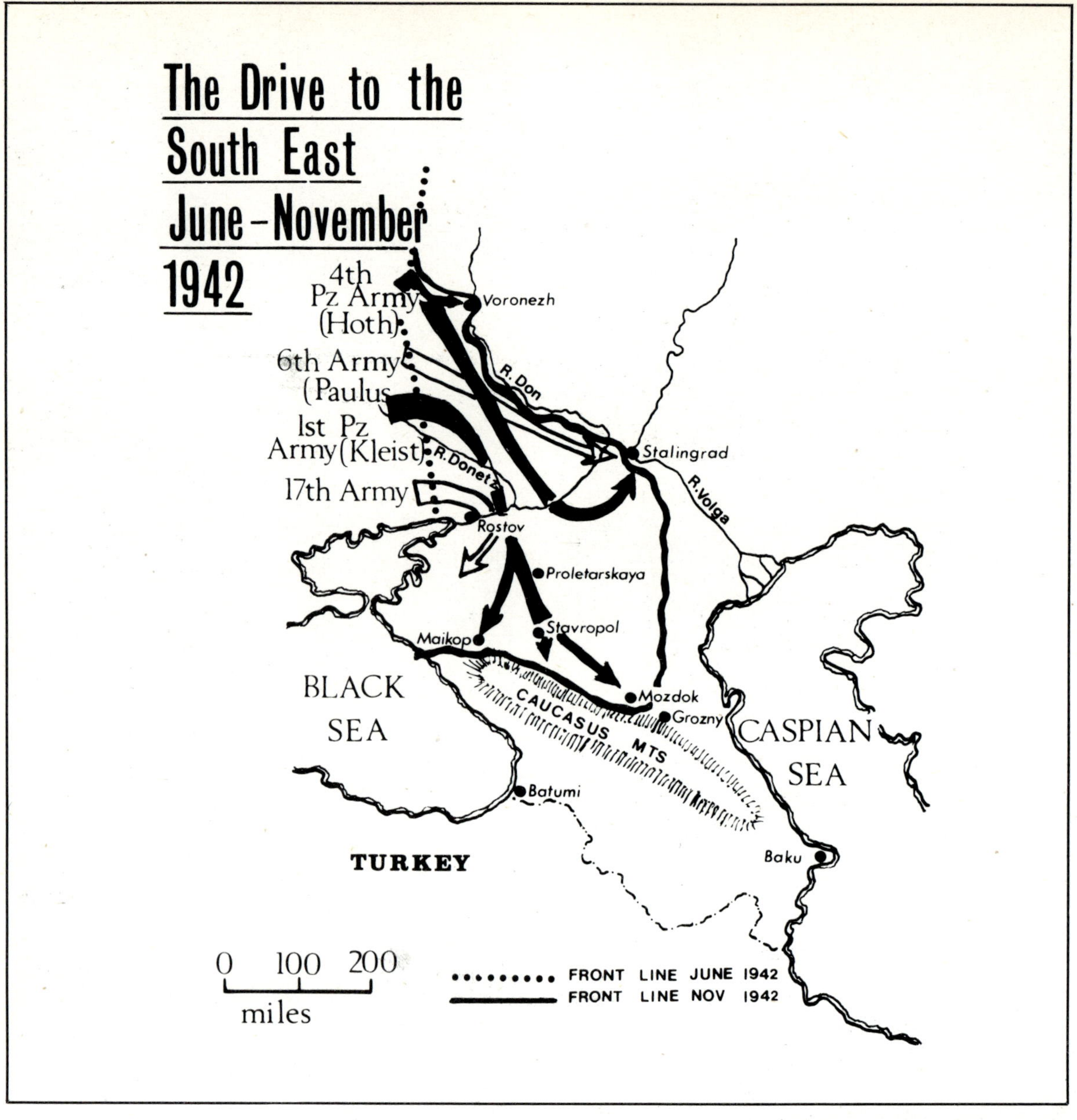

By early summer the German Army was ready to resume the offensive in the centre. Operations in the far south to capture the Crimea were already under way.

Army Group Weichs, which had 4th Panzer Army (Colonel General Hoth) under command, was tasked to break Marshal Timoshenko's defences in the Kursk sector and subsequently to destroy his Army Group against the line of the River Don. This preliminary operation was to provide a springboard for further advances towards Stalingrad and the oil-rich lands of the Caucasus. Hoth, with two Panzer corps and some 800 tanks, was to spearhead the attack. Having achieved the breakthrough, he was to swing right-handed and advance on Stalingrad as Paulus's 6th Army extended along the Don behind him.

The operation, launched on June 28, was a complete success. 4th Panzer Army advanced 120 miles in ten days, battling as it went. This was a classic armoured operation on a big scale. Hoth's orders were clear cut and were not changed. All the available offensive air support was assigned to him, to the exclusion of the slower moving infantry formations. Similarly, a generous allocation of reconnaissance aircraft was put under direct command of his Army. The going was ideal. Huge rolling open plains allowed complete freedom of manoeuvre. The tanks pressed resolutely on, regardless of what was happening on their flanks or of what they had left behind them. These matters were for the follow-up formations and the inherent risks involved were accepted in the interests of maintaining the Army Group aim. Finally, as so often in the past, every General Officer and every subordinate commander was right forward, exerting his personal influence in the very forefront of the battle.

Hardly had 4th Panzer Army reached Voronezh on July 5 than Hoth was re-directed south to support the crossing of the lower Don by Field Marshal von Kleist's 1st Panzer Army, now beginning its advance to the Caucasus. Here was a typical example of the sort of

Colonel General Hoth, commander of 4th Panzer Army.

Field Marshal von Kleist, seen here (right) greeting the commander of Hungarian forces fighting as Germany's allies on the Eastern Front, was in command of 1st Panzer Army that advanced to the Caucasus. In 1940 von Kleist commanded a Panzer Group in the campaign against France and the Low Countries.

ill-informed interference by the Führer's Headquarters which so often drove German commanders in the field to despair. Von Kleist had no need for this support and the additional strain on the routes which the presence of 4th Panzer Army imposed merely slowed up the whole operation. As he remarked at the time, had 4th Panzer Army only been directed onto Stalingrad, the city would have been in German hands by the end of July "without a fight". The whole course of the campaign would then have been altered—indeed, the very outcome might well have been different. In the event, Hoth was directed onto Stalingrad—but too late. At the end of July he was ordered to fight his way north from the lower Don towards Stalingrad, which Paulus's 6th Army was now approaching. By the time he arrived in mid-August the city could no longer be taken "without a fight". It would now have to be stormed. Large numbers of valuable tanks were lost in the subsequent close quarter fighting in the urban area; the lessons of Warsaw had been forgotten.

Meanwhile, 1st Panzer Army made fast time down towards the Caucasus, covering some 200 miles in 11 days. But the troops were becoming exhausted, the tanks

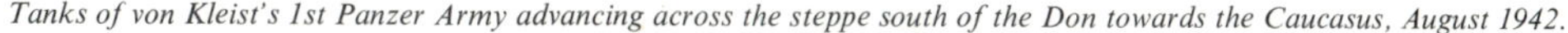

Tanks of von Kleist's 1st Panzer Army advancing across the steppe south of the Don towards the Caucasus, August 1942.

were in grave need of maintenance and fuel had become desperately short. The Army fell prey to a scrappy form of guerilla fighting involving local resistance fighters and the remnants of Russian formations along its supply routes. Von Kleist's lot was made no easier by the removal of his offensive air support to go to Stalingrad. As it reached the Caucasus mountains, the advance gradually dragged to a halt.

In the Stalingrad region, things were to go from bad to worse. In November, a violent Russian counter-offensive fought without regard to human or tank casualties, isolated the city, now held by 6th Army. Despite desperate attempts, in which many Russian tanks were destroyed, 4th Panzer Army, reinforced by LVII Panzer Corps from 1st Panzer Army, was unable to make the breakthrough to relieve Paulus.

CHANGES IN ORGANIZATION

During 1942 the organization of the Panzer Division underwent some significant changes. The dramatic success of the 88mm anti-aircraft gun in the anti-tank rôle led to the introduction of an 88mm battalion into the division. Because of the problems of tank production, the number of tank battalions in each division was reduced to two and the third re-equipped with SP anti-tank guns (Panzerjäger). In consequence, divisions often had as few as 70 or 80 tanks and seldom more than 100. At long last the half-tracked APC (SdKfz 251/1) was produced for one battalion of infantry in each Wehrmacht Panzer Division although SS formations were to receive enough for two. At the same time the designation "Panzergrenadier" was introduced and was generally adopted for all infantry units in Panzer Divisions. The term was later to apply to mechanized infantry divisions also.

The way in which SS formations received preferential treatment over the issue of equipment caused much understandable jealousy. For example, some SS Panzer Divisions had their own organic Tiger units, whilst the Wehrmacht's Tigers were Army troops in independent units. So strong did the rivalry between the two factions become that golden tactical opportunities were to be lost in North-West Europe in 1944 and 1945 through the inequitable issue of fuel and the alleged refusal of some formations to help out their hard-pressed comrades in arms.

GAZALA AND THE FALL OF TOBRUK, 1942

We left the Panzerarmee Afrika facing the British in front of Gazala in the spring of 1942. On May 26, with 333 German and 228 Italian tanks, Rommel advanced by night round the southern extremity of the Gazala position against nearly 900 British tanks, including 167 Grants. The Eighth Army had by now re-equipped with 57mm anti-tank guns and these were well dug in behind extensive minefields. Rommel did enjoy one substantial advantage—the advent of Luftflotte 2 had given him a numerical superiority in the air of 2·5 to 1.

Once again, the British threw away the advantage that their tank strength gave them by over-dispersion and their failure to operate their motorized infantry in sufficiently close co-operation with their armour; this despite Auchinleck's injunction to Ritchie on the subject—"I consider it of the highest importance that you should not break up the organization of either of the armoured divisions. They have been trained to fight as divisions, I hope, and fight as divisions they should." But Ritchie knew best and split them up, with disastrous results.

It goes without saying that, despite the poor overall direction of the British tactical battle, the troops fought magnificently and, in consequence, very heavy casualties were inflicted upon both sides. However, the fundamental difference between them remained. The British, masters of the static defensive battle, possessed neither the ability to regroup nor the flexibility of their opponents. In consequence, opportunity after opportunity to crush the Germans was lost.

Throughout the Gazala battle and those that followed, Rommel was in his element. On May 29 he led the supply echelons of 15th Panzer Division through gaps in the minefields which were inadequately covered by fire; thus saving the Afrika Korps, which was out of fuel and ammunition. On the 30th he led the leading platoon of 21st Panzer Division in a tremendous tussle against the 150 Brigade Box, where the Matildas of 44 RTR covered themselves with glory.

The ding-dong struggle rolled back and forth. No quarter was given or sought. By June 15, after several days hard slogging around the Knightsbridge Box, both sides were nearing exhaustion. Rommel was in his usual precarious logistic state. A fierce fight on the Tobruk-El Adem line resulted in the destruction of several British

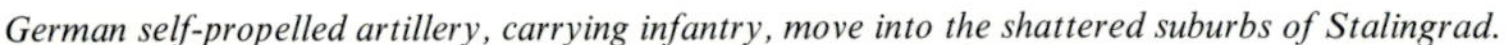

German self-propelled artillery, carrying infantry, move into the shattered suburbs of Stalingrad.

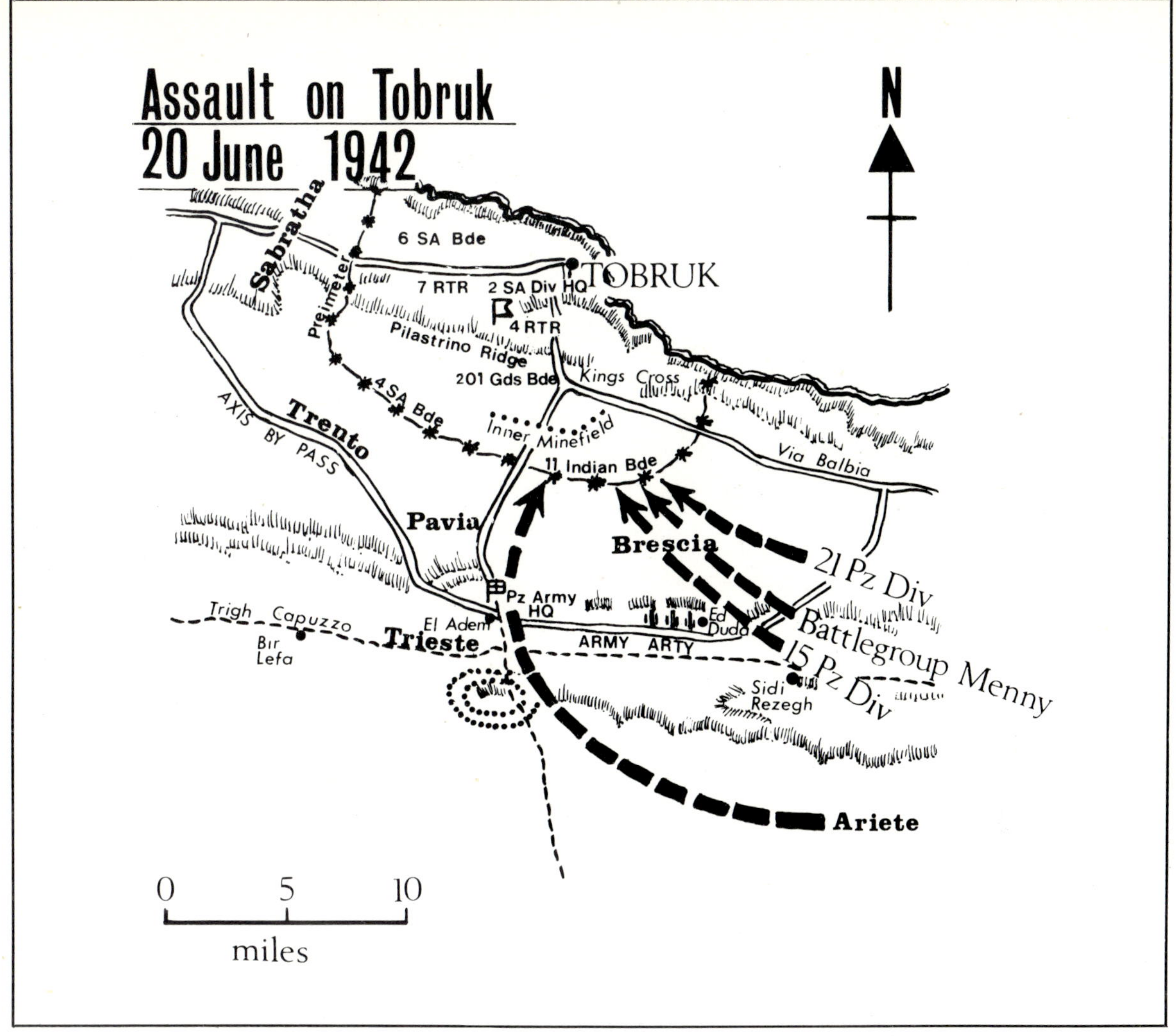

brigades, as Rommel dealt each a concentrated blow. As a result, he was able to acquire vast stocks of British fuel and rations and so restore his administrative balance. Ritchie simply could not get the hang of this desert fighting, despite Auchinleck's plea that he should bring "maximum force into play in the El Adem area. . . . We must emulate the enemy's speed in thought and action. . . ."

On June 20 the Germans broke through the Tobruk perimeter. General Nehring, Commander of the Afrika Korps, and von Bismarck, Commander of 21st Panzer Division, led the assault, the latter riding in a motorcycle sidecar alongside the leading tanks. Rommel, not to be outdone, personally commanded an attack on a 3·7 anti-aircraft battery that was having a devastating effect upon his tanks. On this occasion the 3·7 was shown to rival the 88mm as an anti-tank weapon. But for the stubbornness of the senior Gunners in Cairo, this weapon could have been used with telling success against the Afrika Korps from the earliest days of the campaign. The whole story of the desert war might then have been changed.

Despite the capture of 30,000 prisoners in Tobruk, Rommel was now getting towards the end of his resources. His victory was greeted with great acclaim in Berlin and on the 21st he was promoted Field Marshal. Flushed with success, he fell into his previous error of over-reaching himself. Despite the warnings of Field Marshal Kesselring and of his own loyal staff, he determined to sweep through to the Delta, believing that the British were in a worse plight than he. A resounding victory at Mersa Matruh, giving him a further 8,000 prisoners, seemed to prove his point. However, as he battled forward to the area of the Eighth Army's next defensive position at El Alamein, his strength fell day by day and he outran his air cover. By July 4 the Afrika Korps was down to less than 40 tanks and the soldiers were utterly exhausted. Auchinleck had taken over personal command of the Eighth Army and the British position had stabilized. Somehow, Rommel rallied his troops to resist a series of determined attacks which continued throughout July. It was a real battle of attrition which came very close to sounding the death knell of the Panzerarmee. Had the British armour only been handled better the result could well have been the final eclipse of all Rommel's hopes. As it was, the end of the month saw both armies at a standstill. Auchinleck had saved the day in what the British call First Alamein—but the Germans were still in the fight, despite the sorry state of their Italian allies.

In the Gazala battle very heavy casualties were inflicted on both sides.

THE END IN AFRICA

For the British the next four months were to see them make their first steps towards final victory. For the Germans they were to herald a series of defeats, leading to final collapse.

The arrival of a mass of new equipment in the Delta for the Eighth Army together with a number of fresh divisions from the United Kingdom restored the Army's capacity to carry on the fight and to take the offensive. Furthermore, important changes in command took place. In the middle of August General Alexander replaced Auchinleck and General Montgomery took over command of Eighth Army.

Meanwhile the Royal Navy and the Desert Air Force were having a devastating effect upon the German logistic system, so that even the daily maintenance of the Afrika Korps was a struggle. A battered and weary Panzerarmee, with sickness rife in its ranks after two and a half years hard slogging up and down the Desert and with its equipment suffering badly from lack of spares and replacements, had to face, in Montgomery, a General who had a revitalised force at his disposal and was possessed of the will and ability to win.

Rommel was anxious to withdraw back into Cyrenaica so that he could refurbish and regroup his resources as best he might. But permission to abandon the Alamein position was refused. He therefore decided to take what he saw as the only alternative course—to make a final and determined bid to break through to the Nile. His decision, which was taken in the face of his staff's advice, was largely influenced by a promise from Field Marshal Kesselring to provide him with the petrol he needed.

Both Rommel and Montgomery had appreciated the tactical significance of the Alam Halfa Ridge—a long feature covering the eastern approach to the Alamein position. Even as Rommel waited for the moon to be right for a night operation, Montgomery prepared to defend it.

On August 31, 1942, under a full moon, the Panzerarmee broke into the minefields in the south near Qaret el Himeimat. Of the 200 German tanks available 27 were Panzer IV F2, the new "Mark IV Special" with its long 75mm gun. The going was softer than expected and a number of unidentified minefields were encountered. As a result, surprise was lost and the rate of advance slowed down severely. When daylight came the Axis troops were advancing slowly towards the Ridge where a mixed force of British Grants, Crusaders and 37mm Stuarts lay in wait.

As the range closed a fierce fire-fight ensued in which the new Mark IV's and Rommels supporting Stukas played an important part. But the attack was held. By evening the Panzerarmee was halted and almost out of petrol—the sinking of a precious tanker in Tobruk by the Royal Navy had done much to see to that.

Throughout September 2 the Desert Air Force and the British guns hammered away so that by the 3rd the Axis troops were in full retreat, having suffered heavy losses of men and material. By the morning of the 6th Rommel had regrouped on the western edge of the great mine barrier, managing to retain control of the gaps in the south through which he had passed. The weeks that followed saw the Germans spread thinly along the Alamein position, interspersed with their Italian allies. Nowhere were they able to form a sizeable counter-attack force. Rommel's health forced him to return home on sick leave whilst his troops waited grimly but without hope to face Montgomery's inevitable onslaught.

When the blow fell on October 23 the result was almost inevitable. Despite heroic resistance, the Germans were ground down by the sheer weight of the artillery fire and air attacks which characterized the next ten days. Montgomery had deliberately bided his time until he was thoroughly ready. 300 of the new Sherman tanks had arrived in his armoured formations and the troops had been retrained.

Rommel returned to command in the battle but even his ability was no substitute for the imbalance in strength with which he had to contend. The British paid a heavy price in tanks and men for their victory but it did not compare in relative terms with the cost to the Germans and Italians. So fierce had been the bombardment that virtually all their anti-tank guns were destroyed—enabling the British tanks, as they broke out, to engage those of the Axis at long range and pick them off.

Thanks to a combination of his own skill and Montgomery's caution and greatly aided by a sudden storm of torrential rain, Rommel managed to disengage on the night of November 7 and fall back to Sollum, leaving 450 out of his original 600 tanks on the battlefield.

The writing was now on the wall. Though still a very sick man, Rommel fought a brilliant withdrawal along the coast into Tunisia, with Montgomery hard on his heels. It is interesting to find that in the battle of Medenine Rommel lost no less than 50 tanks without inflicting a single loss on his opponents. This was mainly due to the fact that the British had now introduced yet another anti-tank gun, the 17-pdr. (76·2mm), to supplement the 57mm and Montgomery had clearly learned how to handle it.

On November 8, 1942 the Allies invaded North Africa and the Axis forces were caught between two fires. Despite the introduction of a handful of Tiger tanks and the effectiveness of Panzer IV F2, particularly against the inexperienced troops under General Eisenhower, capitulation was inevitable. Hundreds of battle-tried and highly skilled tank-crewmen went into captivity. Their loss was a serious blow for the Wehrmacht. By May 13, 1943 the fight for North Africa was over and an historic era in the development of armoured warfare had ended.

The new "Mark IV Specials"—as the British called them—though few in number played an important part in the fierce fire-fight at Alam Halfa. They were armed with the long 7,5cm KwK 40 L/43.

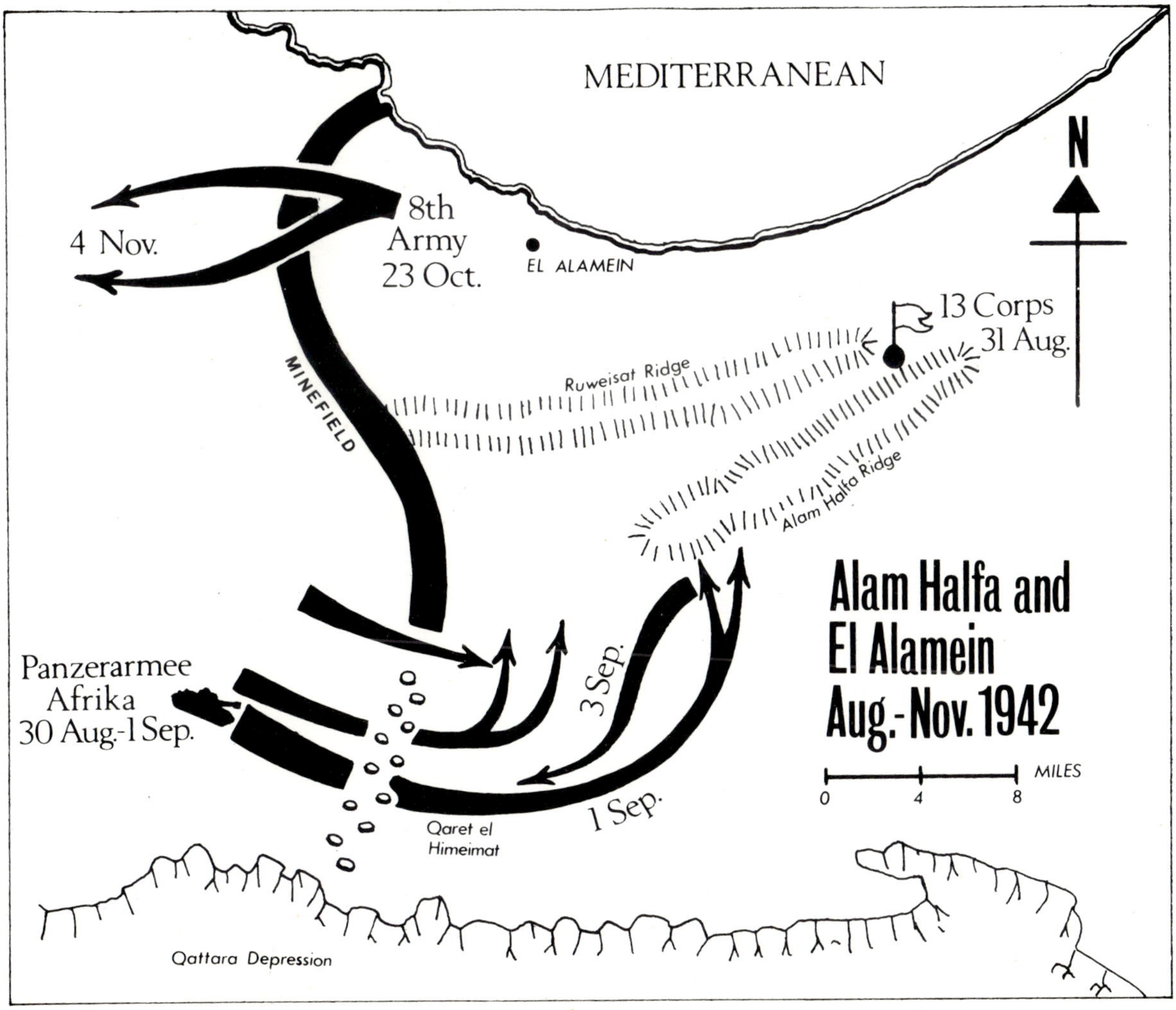

Alam Halfa and El Alamein Aug.-Nov. 1942

MEDITERRANEAN

N

8th Army 23 Oct.

4 Nov.

EL ALAMEIN

13 Corps 31 Aug.

MINEFIELD

Ruweisat Ridge

Alam Halfa Ridge

Panzerarmee Afrika 30 Aug.-1 Sep.

3 Sep.

1 Sep.

Qaret el Himeimat

Qattara Depression

MILES 0 4 8

1943—THE TURNING POINT

1943 was to mark the turning point of the war for the Germans. The magnitude of the disasters at Stalingrad in February and of Operation Citadel in the Kursk Salient in July ensured that all hopes of final victory had disappeared.

Even as F.M. Paulus's 6th Army was making its last heroic stand, at a cost of some 140,000 dead and 90,000 prisoners, huge Russian forces were sweeping von Kleist's 1st Panzer Army out of the Caucasus. The Germans continued to strike blow after blow at the flood-tide that was overwhelming their whole front, but their numbers were dwindling steadily and their resources were almost spent. Faith in the High Command had gone. Only the quality of their leadership, their patriotism and high sense of military dedication kept the armies going.

In the midst of all these difficulties, von Manstein, now commanding Army Group Don, somehow persuaded Hitler to allow him to make a limited tactical withdrawal in order to regroup 1st and 4th Panzer Armies. This done, he launched a brilliant counter-stroke against a force eight times the size of his own. By concentrating his 350 tanks, he achieved a seven to one majority at the Schwerpunkt of his attack and broke clean through to the Donetz, shattering the opposition and inflicting enormous casualties. Surprise and clear-cut directives, giving freedom for tactical judgement and the relief of responsibility for the flanks, enabled commanders to concentrate on the crucial business of leading their formations and of maintaining the aim of the operation. Had the weather only held for a little longer, there is no telling what the scale of von Manstein's success might have been. But the thaw set in and General Mud took over from General Winter. The whole battlefield became a morass in which both sides were left wallowing and all further fighting became impossible.

The British first encountered the Tiger in Tunisia in February 1943. Having had news of the tanks' arrival through a prison camp "leak" they were prepared for them. This Tiger was knocked out at Kournine.

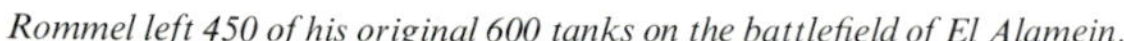

Rommel left 450 of his original 600 tanks on the battlefield of El Alamein.

General Winter in command. Panzer III with German infantry near Rostov in February 1943.

General Mud takes over from General Winter.

GUDERIAN RECALLED

Back in Germany a remarkable situation had arisen. Early in February, the higher echelons of the OKW had at last realized that they had lost the confidence of the field armies and that the once magnificent armoured force was at its last gasp. Commanders were calling for a man with great experience of armour and of command in battle to resurrect their panzer formations. In a spell of unusual lucidity and, possibly, of near despair, Hitler put his pride in his pocket, realizing that only Guderian could meet this heavy challenge. He sent for him on February 17 and offered to reinstate him in the Army as Inspector General of Armoured Troops. It was a huge and daunting task, embracing every aspect of the organization, training and equipment of armoured units and formations. At Guderian's insistence, he was given the status of an Army Commander and directly subordinated to Hitler himself. (An almost entirely similar situation had arisen earlier in England when General Hobart, whom Guderian so admired, had been brought back by Churchill and offered the chance to put British armour on its feet. Hobart insisted that whoever did so would need a seat on the Army Council—but even the exigencies of war failed to break down the conventionalism of Whitehall and he had to decline the job, taking over a new armoured division instead.)

Guderian's remit was wide and he was even given powers over the Waffen SS and Luftwaffe armoured formations on matters of training and organization. Armed with this directive, Guderian made a rapid appreciation and presented his findings to Hitler and the assembled General Staff on March 9. So desperate was the overall situation that he had as his aim for 1943 the provision of "a certain number of Panzer Divisions with complete combat efficiency, capable of making limited objective attacks."[1] The qualification is highly signifi-

[1] Guderian "Panzer Leader", p. 295.

In February 1943 Guderian was recalled by Hitler and appointed Inspector-General of Armoured Troops.

cant. For 1944 he sought to create divisions capable of large scale operations, each equipped with some 400 tanks and supporting arms in proportion. Far better, he urged, to have a few, well balanced, strong divisions than many only partly equipped.

What a contrast these proposals made to the policies of the High Command since 1940, which had so emasculated divisions in order to pander to Hitler's insane love of large numbers of formations, entirely ignoring the appalling waste of manpower and misuse of precious equipment that inevitably ensued; quite apart from the fact that it cut clean across the tactical requirement for the concentration of armour and for the balance that had been demanded by all their expert advisers since Panzer Divisions were first established.

Whilst stressing the need to improve the reliability of Panther, Guderian emphasized the importance of keeping up the production rate of the well-tried Panzer IV, provided that it did not affect that of Tiger and Panther. In this he was wise. We have already seen that, in spite of newer models, Panzer IV was to remain the German Army's workhorse for the rest of the war. With the recent disastrous introduction of Tiger clearly in mind, he demanded that future new equipment should be introduced into battle properly—in sufficient numbers and at the right time, under the right conditions. He proposed better crew training (including participation in the final assembly of their tanks), the provision of adequate scales of training ammunition and equipment and of sufficient time to train, without the customary interference of making units under training move from one area to another. Only carefully selected and experienced commanders were acceptable to him and new formations were to be built on cadres of battle-experienced troops, specially withdrawn from the field for this purpose. Reconnaissance units were to be resurrected and a new reconnaissance vehicle, based on existing assemblies, provided. (Here spoke his own experience in Poland and France. In Russia, reconnaissance units had almost disappeared). As so often before, he made the case for more armoured half-tracks for the Panzer grenadiers, stressing the importance of their rôle; he called for more self-propelled artillery and SP anti-tank guns in the Panzer Division and finally proposed that secondary theatres should be made to manage with second class equipment if need be.

It was a tour de force and, for a man who had been eating his heart out in despair for over a year, a performance of such quality that only a superb professional could have produced it in the circumstances. No-one today would challenge any of his proposals and they were received with enthusiasm by his audience, who saw with relief that here, at last, was the man who would shoulder their burdens and assume the responsibilities that they had so shamefully mishandled. Despite the success of his presentation, Guderian found himself once more locked in combat with the Gunners, who objected to his plans for the control of SP anti-tank guns and assault guns, which they felt must remain with the artillery. On this point alone, Guderian was over-ruled, only for Hitler to acknowledge nine months later that he had made a mistake. By then the die was cast and it was too late.

Months of furious activity followed, during which near miracles of reorganization and re-equipment were achieved. The new Panzerjäger 38(t) "Hetzer" came into widespread use, spaced armour was provided for the few remaining Panzer III and for Panzer IV, to defeat the Russians' hollow charged ammunition, whilst the frontal armour of both Panther and Panzer IV was increased to 100mm.

Porsche's Tiger (known as Elefant) was now coming into service. Lacking a coaxial machine-gun for close-quarter fighting, it was really an SP anti-tank gun rather than a tank. Guderian condemned it as such. However, some 90 of these cumbersome machines were produced and had to be used. They were formed into two battalions and used in Operation Citadel in Model's 9th Army. Their limitations were quickly exposed and the majority were knocked out early in the battle. For the very reasons that he had rejected Elefant, Guderian also rejected the wooden mock-up of Porsche's Maus. Turreted though it was, this monster, whose all-up weight now looked as if it would approach 200 tons, was to carry no machine-guns for close-range fighting. Two of these giants reached the trial stage, but they never came into service.

Meanwhile, Panzer IV production was continuing at an average of about 200 a month, Panther production was approaching that figure, and Tiger production brought the overall monthly tank output up to about 500. In view of the weight of the Allied aerial attacks on industrial centres and the multifarious other vehicles and SP guns being produced simultaneously, these figures were

Porsche's Panzerjaeger Tiger, originally called Ferdinand (after Porsche) and then re-named Elefant. It was simply a conversion of the original Porsche Tiger tank design to a self-propelled anti-tank weapon. It fought in Operation Citadel, on other parts of the Eastern front, and then in Italy. This vehicle has the additional protection in front of the gun mantlet which was a retrospective modification made after experience in the field.

remarkable. In part they were the result of foresight, which had led to the establishment of factories in the heart of Austria, out of range of the bombers. Panther was still giving a lot of trouble. Guderian was far from happy about its transmission and suspension, whilst its optics, too, were unsatisfactory. Hitler was desperate to get his new toy into action, against all advice.

KURSK

Ever since the end of von Manstein's counterstroke earlier in the year, the Germans had been containing a large pocket of Russians in the salient opposite Kursk. Von Manstein was eager to mount a fresh attack to eliminate it before the enemy had time to consolidate but, although he agreed the need, Hitler would not agree the timing. He was determined to get Panther into battle and the operation was to wait until Panthers were available in strength. Guderian, bearing in mind his limited aims for 1943, was never keen on becoming involved at Kursk and begged Hitler to call the whole idea off. He knew that the Army simply could not afford the price in tanks and trained soldiers that would have to be paid. Whilst Hitler admitted that he had misgivings, he allowed himself to be persuaded by Keitel and Zeitzler, his senior advisers, and announced that the plan would go forward as soon as Panther was ready. June came and von Manstein himself approached the Führer to press for cancellation. The Russians had made extensive defensive preparations, surprise was lost, and the Wehrmacht was faced with a battle on ground of the enemy's choosing with no room to manoeuvre. The defensive minefields that the Russians had prepared were now many miles deep and countless strongpoints had been constructed. Hitler was implacable. On July 4 Hoth's 4th Panzer Army of 18 divisions (including 10 armoured) attacked from the south whilst Model with 9th Army, also of 18 divisions (seven of them armoured), attacked simultaneously from the north. It was the greatest armoured battle of all time—described by General Strawson as "Alam Halfa blown up 1,000 times."[1]

A tremendous slogging match ensued. Torrential rain turned much of the southern flank into a bog. The going was terribly slow. In the north, 9th Army bogged down after six miles. 4th Panzer Army battled resolutely on, knocking out some 2,000 tanks and a similar number of guns, whilst taking 32,000 prisoners. But it was like hitting a sponge. The German losses were very heavy. Finally, on July 13, Hitler called off the operation when he heard that the Allies had landed in Sicily; a curious excuse for his own utter failure as Commander in Chief to appreciate the price his Army was paying for his stubbornness. The Russians had by this time built up the Red Army to mammoth proportions and were able

[1] Strawson "Hitler as Military Commander", p. 176.

Von Manstein, seen here (centre) inspecting the positions of a Panzergrenadier Regiment in June 1943, pressed Hitler to cancel Operation Citadel. Previously he had been eager to mount an attack that would eliminate the Kursk salient. (B.L.Davis)

Operation Citadel—the Battle of Kursk—begins. On July 4, 1943, thirty-six German divisions, including 17 Panzer Divisions, began a pincer movement against the Kursk salient.

to replace their casualties as fast as they were incurred. Even as they mounted their counter-attack in the salient, they launched two simultaneous assaults between Bryansk and Orel, making deep penetrations. They had seized the initiative and the Germans were never to recover it.

The Red Army facing the Germans at Kursk was a very different proposition to the brave but ill-trained and un-co-ordinated horde that faced them in 1941. The salient had been brilliantly prepared for defence. A complex pattern of well camouflaged strongpoints, based upon groups of anti-tank guns protected by minefields and sited to a depth of over 12 miles had been organised across the front. Known to the Germans as "Pakfronts", these strongpoints called for a new tactical concept to deal with them. Up to 10 guns would open up on a single tank at short range. The Russian fire discipline was exemplary. Very often the first indication of the existence of one of these concealed positions was the destruction of a leading tank by fire or the explosion of a mine beneath its tracks. A single German corps would sometimes lift as many as 40,000 mines in one day.

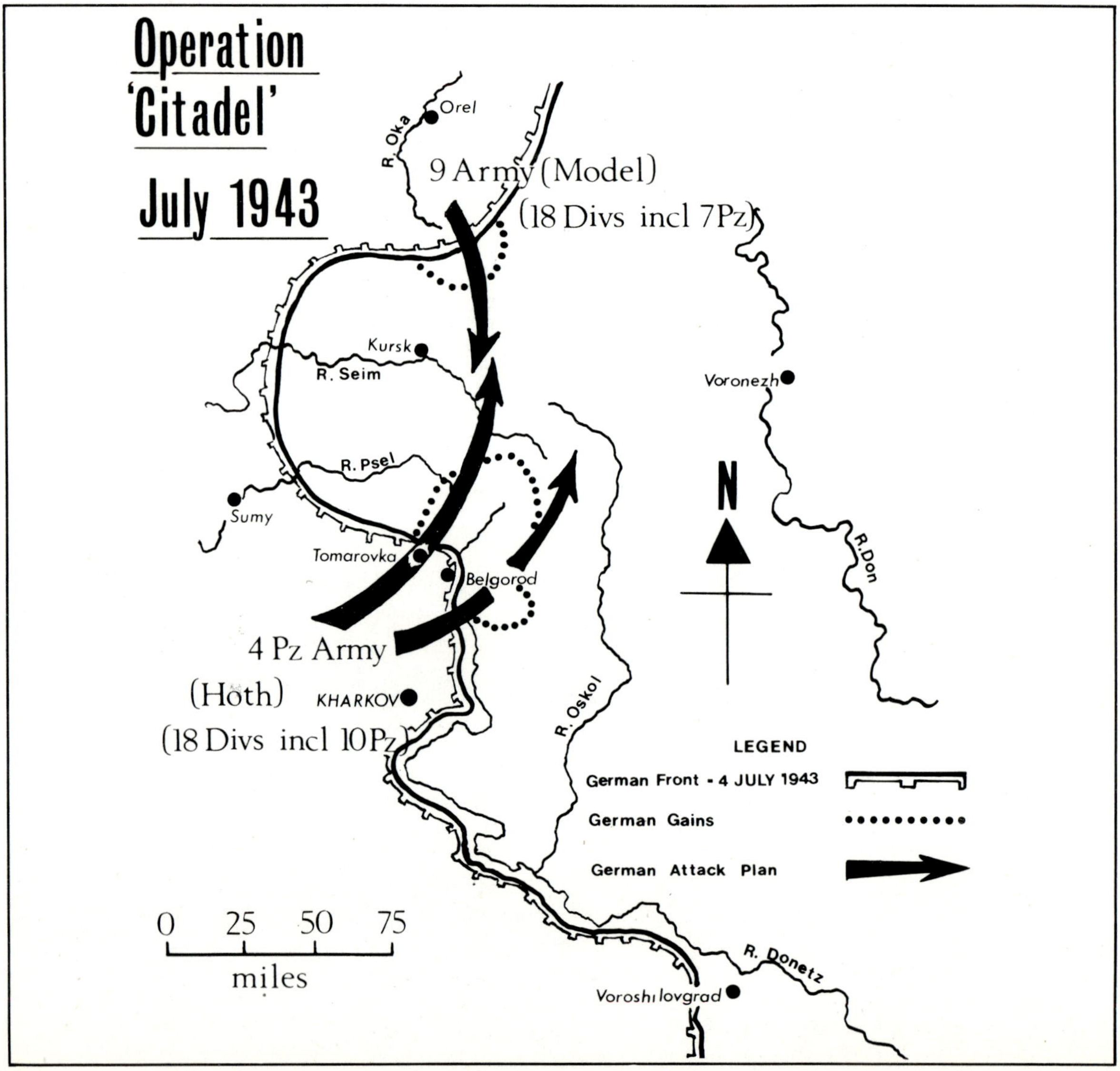

Operation 'Citadel' July 1943

Orel
R. Oka
9 Army (Model)
(18 Divs incl 7Pz)
Kursk
R. Seim
Voronezh
R. Psel
Sumy
N
R. Don
Tomarovka
Belgorod
4 Pz Army
(Hoth)
KHARKOV
(18 Divs incl 10Pz)
R. Oskol
LEGEND
German Front - 4 JULY 1943
German Gains
German Attack Plan
0 25 50 75
miles
R. Donetz
Voroshilovgrad

The Battle of Kursk was the greatest armoured battle of all time.

TACTICAL TECHNIQUES

The Panzer Divisions developed a formation known as a "Panzerkeil". This was a wedge, spearheaded by heavy tanks to bludgeon a path into the position, with medium and light tanks echeloned off to the flanks. This technique was elaborated to the "Panzerglocke", a bell-shape, with armoured engineers following up the leading Tigers or Panthers. As before, medium tanks covered the flanks. A command group came close behind the engineers to control both the tanks and the supporting bombers. Light tanks filled the mouth of the bell, ready to develop the pursuit if need be.

Although regarded with some trepidation, attacks were made with marked success at night—but only when the going and weather were suitable, the standard of training of the troops was sufficiently high, and a daylight reconnaissance had been possible. In addition it was found to be essential for clearly defined features to exist, such as a road or track, to mark the axis of the advance. When available, direction-finding equipment was also employed. Since the whole formation moved closed-up it is easy to understand the need for a high standard of training. Losses at night were usually slight, so the dividend was a handsome one.

In general, success against "Pakfronts" depended upon:

a. Adequate reconnaissance
b. Good ground-to-air communications
c. A high state of tank gunnery
d. Maintenance of momentum, with the tanks halting only to fire
e. The correct positioning of Forward Observers for all supporting weapons
f. The practice of holding reserves of fuel and ammunition, carried in armoured vehicles, close behind the fighting echelons
g. The skilful use of white and coloured tank smoke for screening and marking.

In his book "Panzer Battles", von Mellenthin asserts that the flower of the German Army fell at Kursk but that "the fierce resolution of the fighting troops remained unshaken."[1] That this was so is borne out by the series of successful actions fought by elements of General Balck's XLVIII Panzer Corps (part of 4th Panzer Army) over the coming months. On August 20, a battle-group of some 20 tanks, a Panzergrenadier battalion and a reconnaissance company, together with a handful of guns, all under the command of Colonel von Natzmer, the 1a of Panzergrenadier Division Gross Deutschland, pushed back an entire Russian armoured corps and an

[1] Von Mellenthin "Panzer Battles", p. 230.

A German armoured column moves up to the battle-front in Operation Citadel as Stukas return to base. Nothing could break the Russian defence, and on July 13 the offensive was called off as the Russian counter-offensive in its turn took over command of the battlefield.

The Jagdpanther with its 88mm gun had an outstanding success in battle, especially in North-West Europe.

infantry division at Akhtyrka. Tactical surprise and skilful handling of the tanks won the day.

In the months that followed, Balck's inspiring leadership and innate tactical skill met with success after success. In November, a major attack by his Corps in the Kiev Salient, involving some six Panzer Divisions, destroyed over 150 tanks, 320 assorted artillery pieces and 3,000 men.

TECHNICAL ACHIEVEMENT

Meanwhile, back in Germany, Guderian was hard at work. Amidst much speculation over Hitler's fantastic ideas on super-heavy tanks, the Gunners made a bid to get production of Panzer IV stopped, in order to divert industrial effort to the manufacture of self-propelled guns. After hard battling, this stupid proposition was foiled by Guderian. The loss of the Panzer IV production would have been disastrous to his strenuous efforts to rebuild the Army's armoured strength. Panther was by no means cured of its ills and Panzer IV was still the principal tank in service. At this time a superb armoured car, the Puma (SdKfz 234/2), powered by a diesel engine and mounting a high velocity 50mm KwK L/60 gun in its turret, had become available. Originally intended for desert use, it had now appeared too late.

On October 20, the pilot model of the Jagdpanther was shown to Hitler. In January 1944 it was in production! This magnificent SP anti-tank gun was to have outstanding success in battle and to pose many problems for the armoured units of the Allies in the struggle for North-West Europe. On October 24, four days later, the wooden mock-ups of Tiger B (often called the King Tiger) and Jagdtiger (on the same chassis as Tiger B) were also demonstrated. It was to be only two months from this date that the first production model of Tiger B came off the stocks. Technical achievements of this magnitude are hard to believe even today. When one considers the circumstances under which they occurred, the facts become even more incredible. During the same winter, the first trials of the running gear for Maus were taking place—clearly it took far more than Guderian's rejection of the concept to dissuade Hitler or his friend Dr Porsche!

FIGHTING WITHDRAWAL

In September 1943, Italy had capitulated and, as in Russia, the Germans were fighting a desperate but offensive rearguard action there with considerable skill. Another winter came and went on the Eastern Front, with all that this meant in terms of logistic difficulty and human suffering for the armour. The soldiers fought on with grim determination. Although the Red Army was by now becoming increasingly well trained and equipped, the German commanders were continuing to use their tanks with telling effect when the opportunity offered. In May 1944 von Manteuffel's Gross Deutschland Division counter-attacked a massive breakthrough at Jassy, just inside the Rumanian frontier. At the cost of only 11 tanks to himself, von Manteuffel hit the Russians so hard that only 60 Russian tanks escaped. This was his first encounter with the Joseph Stalin heavy tank and it made a great impression on him. It was proof against the 88mm at 2,200 metres and this range had to be halved to ensure a knock-out. Yet the fact remains that the Germans' superiority in tactical handling and greater flexibility continued to give them local successes. Talking to Liddell Hart after the war about this engagement, von Manteuffel remarked "In a tank battle, if you stand still you are lost".[1]

Barely a month later, on June 6, the Allies invaded Normandy. The last phase of the battle for the defence of the Fatherland had begun. With three campaigns on their hands, every tank the Germans could muster was needed in the field.

JUNE 1944—NORMANDY

Of the sixty German divisions in the West in June 1944 ten were armoured. Despite the casualties suffered on the Eastern Front and the incessant drain these imposed upon German resources of tank crews and vehicles, the three divisions of 1 SS Panzer Corps (21st Panzer, Panzer Lehr and 12th SS Panzer (Hitler Jugend)) which were covering the invasion area were in good order, well equipped and had high morale. Furthermore, in accordance with Guderian's policy, their commanders were battle-tried and of good quality. The Corps Commander was Sepp Dietrich and the Army Group Commander Erwin Rommel. The remaining seven panzer divisions were in Panzergruppe West under the direct control of

[1] Liddell Hart "The Other Side of the Hill".

Field Marshal von Runstedt, the Commander-in-Chief West.

By this time both Tiger E and Panther were available in some strength. A few Tiger B were also to be found on this front. As the campaign developed, growing numbers of Jagdpanther strengthened the Germans' tank destroying capability. Given a free hand, von Runstedt and Rommel should have inflicted heavy punishment on the Allies, despite the fact that they disagreed on the method to be employed. But the control from Berlin was so tight and the latitude allowed to commanders in the field so limited that every tried principle of armoured warfare went by the board, with divisions being committed piecemeal and ultimately destroyed in detail in many cases. Nevertheless, the tremendous hitting power of the German tanks and the character of the close bocage country, which cut fighting ranges to a few hundred yards at the most, cost the invaders dear. However, it was now the Allies turn to enjoy absolute air superiority. The effect this had upon the movement of reinforcing divisions was devastating, both in terms of delay and of casualties. Troops on the battlefield were under constant air attack from fighters throughout the hours of daylight and frequently bombed at night.

On July 17 Rommel's car was attacked from the air and the Field Marshal was severely wounded. So ended the fighting career of one of Germany's outstanding "panzer leaders" and one who had made a major contribution to the development of mobile warfare. On the next day, a curiously inept attack by three British armoured divisions east of Caen, known as "Operation Goodwood", was heavily defeated by a smallish force of well deployed tanks and anti-tank guns sited on the dominating Bourguebus ridge. Over 300 British tanks were destroyed. Whilst this operation achieved one of its primary aims, in that it drew the bulk of the German armour onto the Caen "hinge", enabling the US 1st Army to break out of the bridgehead on the west, its conduct ran counter to every tried principle and a heavy price had to be paid in consequence. Despite the protests

Winter on the Eastern Front.

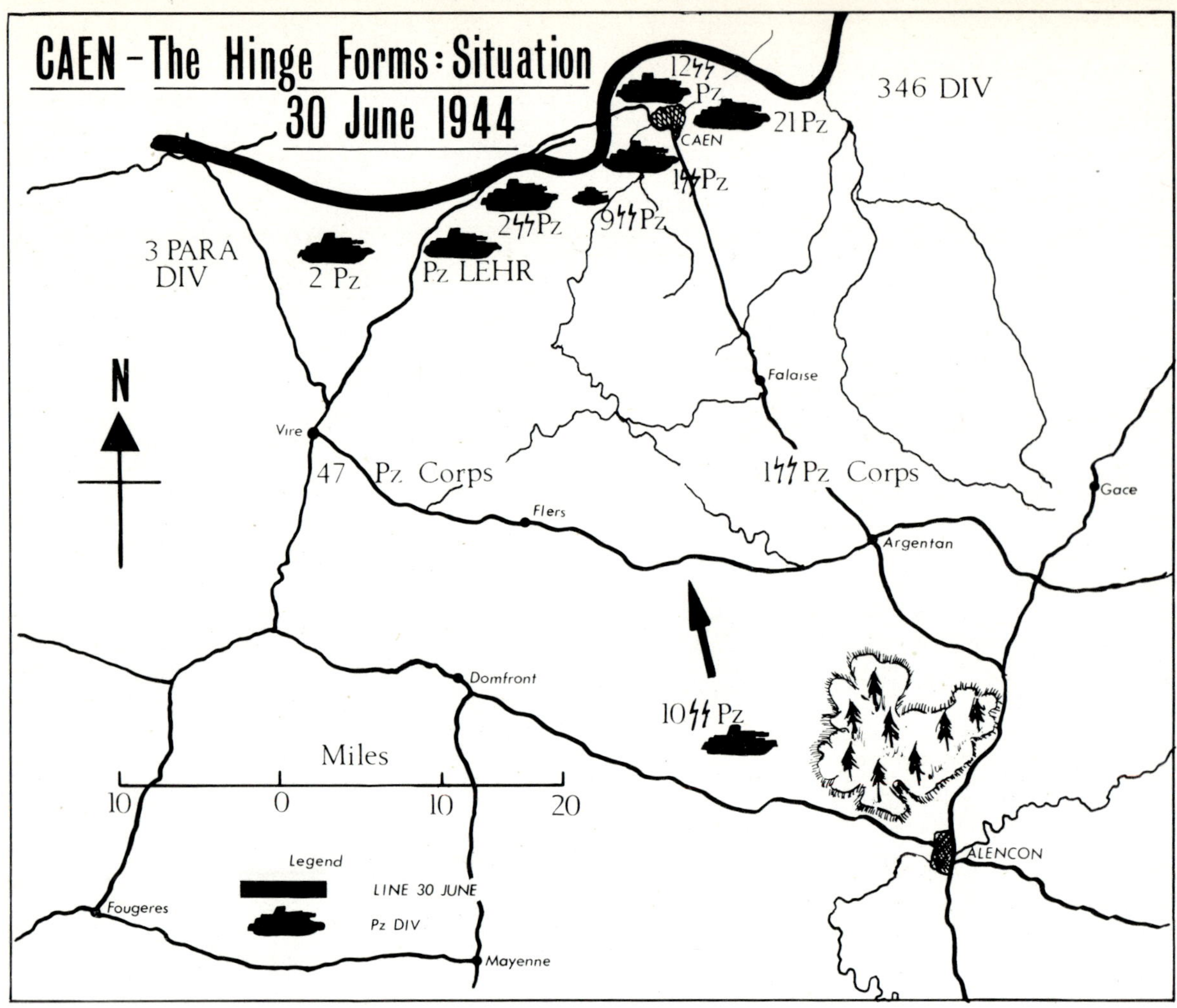

of General Roberts of 11th Armoured Division, the tanks were largely shorn of their infantry and had to advance on a one squadron front in the wake of a pulverizing aerial bombardment. Under devastating anti-tank fire, the advance came to a halt. As the day wore on the German position was reinforced and deepened and, with darkness, the divisions had to limp off the battlefield to reorganize. The initial effect of the bombing had been stunning. Tiger tanks were turned upside down by the blast, but the Germans fought on, demonstrating once again the strength of their fighting spirit.

The victory was short-lived. Within weeks the disastrous defeats of Falaise and of Hitler's ill-judged counter-stroke towards Avranches reduced the German armoured formations to near annihilation. Only scattered remnants escaped in the great retreat across the Seine. No further major armoured engagement was to be fought in the West until the Führer's last desperate gamble in the Ardennes in December.

As part of the aftermath of the assassination attempt on Hitler on July 20, Guderian, still struggling to keep the battered armoured force in being, was appointed Chief of the General Staff—an ironical development in the face of his earlier disgrace and fall from favour. Whatever conclusions may be drawn from this apparent capitulation to the will of a man whom he had almost openly derided, no-one can deny the scale of the achievements of this highly professional and dedicated soldier during a period of more than 20 years devotion to the cause of armour and his country.

JUNE 1944—THE RUSSIANS ADVANCE

Even as the battle of the Normandy bridgehead was raging, the Russians were breaking through on the Central Front. Their main attack was launched on June 22 with 146 infantry divisions and 43 tank brigades. In their efforts to stem the tide, the Germans lost 25 divisions. Some 80,000 men were taken prisoner. Despite the measure of this disaster, the high professional skill of their commanders never left them—nor did their determination to fight on. Between August 5 and 9 General Balck, now commanding 4th Panzer Army, mounted a telling counterstroke against two Russian bridgeheads across the Vistula in the general area of Baranov. Realizing the need to conserve his limited manpower, he made maximum use of concentrated artillery fire and massed assault guns to support a force of only six tank battalions. Demonstrating, once again, his ability to regroup at will and so to bring superior force to bear at a given point, deliberately reducing his strength

By the time of the Allied landings in Normandy the Panther's teething troubles were long since over and this most formidable tank was available in some strength.

elsewhere to dangerous proportions, Balck inflicted so heavy a defeat on the Russians that the advance was halted and disaster averted.

The great bulk of the German armour was now committed in the East. Nevertheless, well handled groups of tanks and SP guns were to impose very serious delays upon the Allies' advance through France, Belgium and Holland.

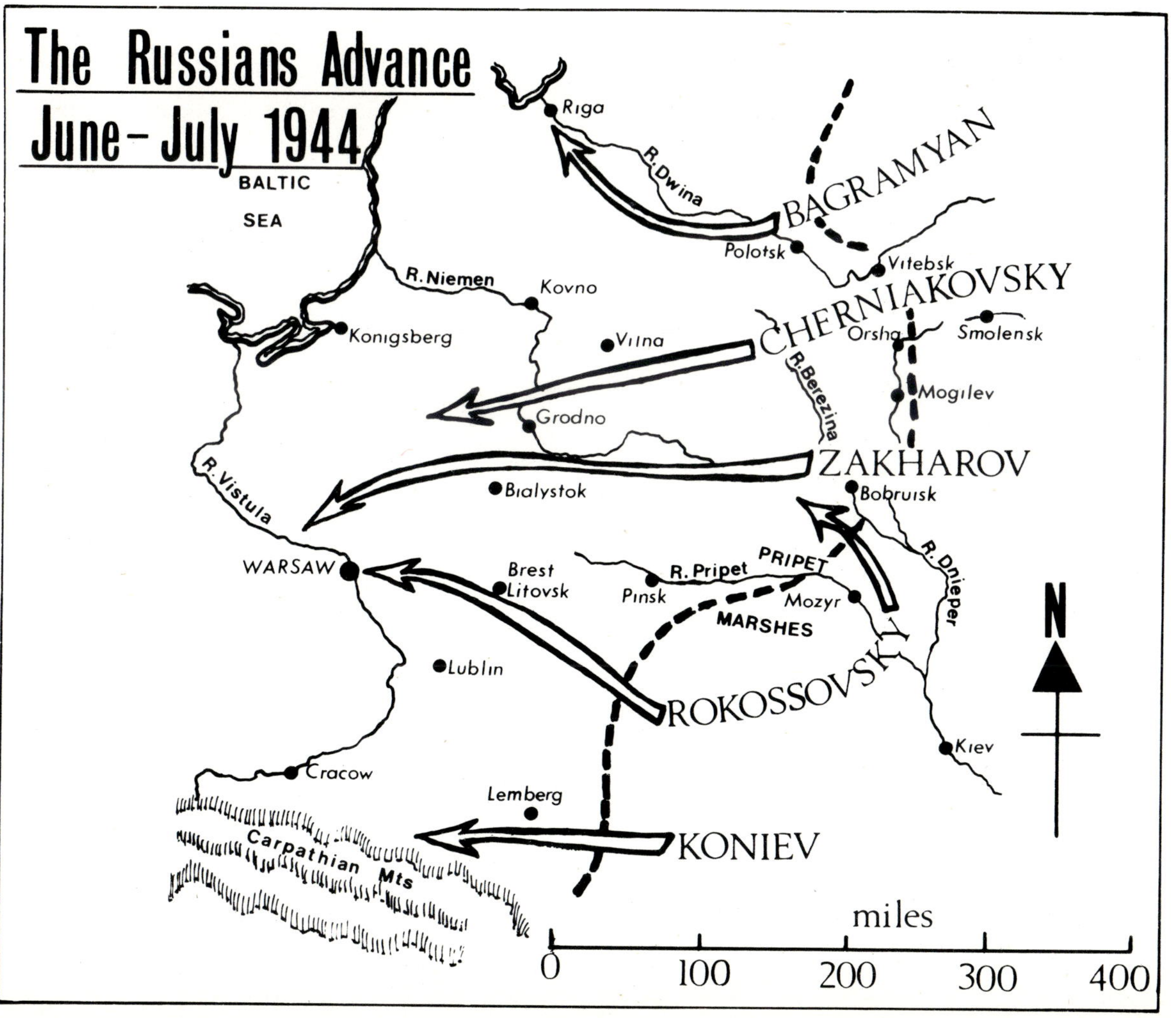

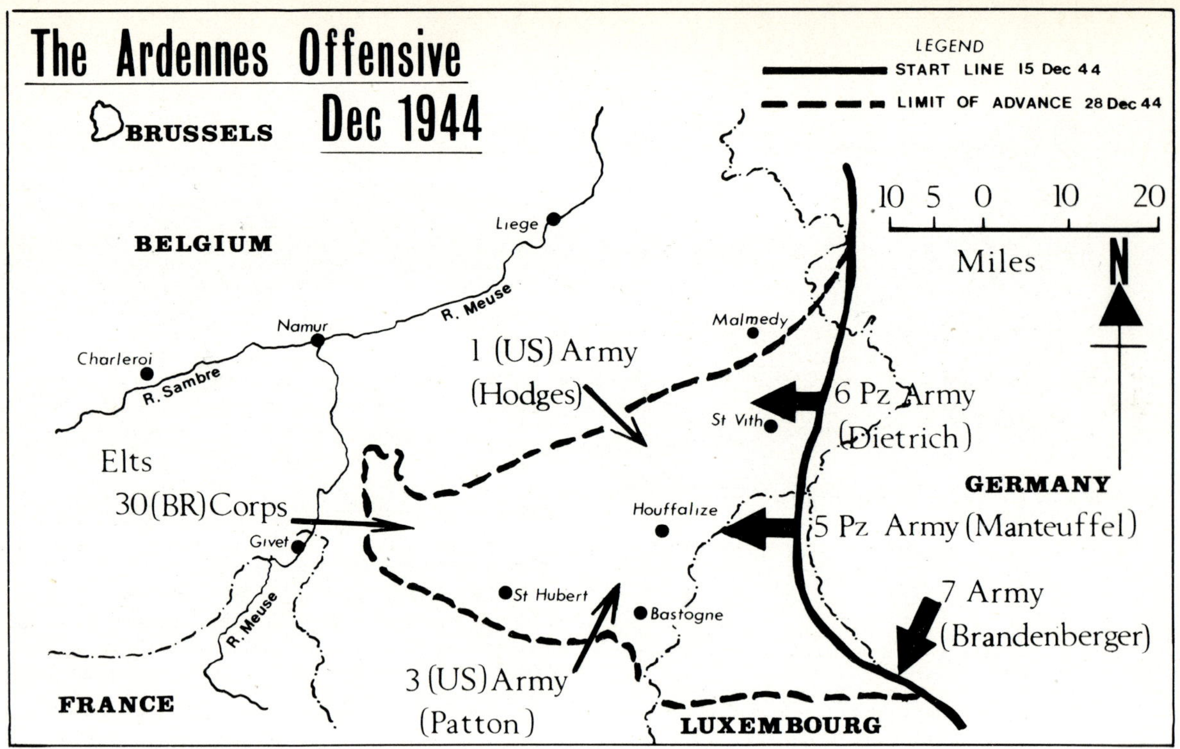

HITLER'S LAST THROW— THE ARDENNES

Although defeat was staring him in the face, Hitler determined to make a final effort in the West to split Eisenhower's forces and so buy some time. Recalling von Runstedt, who had been disgraced after the early set-backs in Normandy, and gathering together every tank and every soldier he could raise, Hitler formed a force of ten well-equipped Panzer Divisions and some twenty infantry divisions to attack the Americans' positions in the Ardennes on December 16. Surprise, aided by bad weather, paid off dramatically for the first few hours. However, the terrain, the determination of some of the American units and an uncharacteristic German failure to exploit areas of success, all combined with the setting of an over-ambitious aim, ensured that von Runstedt failed to reach his first major objective, the River Meuse, on time. After some of the hardest fighting of the war, the front was stabilized. By January 2 the battle was lost, at a terrible cost to the German Army. Whilst the Offensive reduced the Allies' effective fighting strength by ten per cent and resulted in the loss of some thousands of tanks and other vehicles, the almost bottomless well of American industry was able to make good all the material damage in two weeks. For the Germans, the loss of some 130,000 men killed and wounded was an almost irreparable blow. 6th SS Panzer Army alone had lost 37,000 men and between 300 and 400 tanks. 5th Panzer Army, under von Manteuffel, lost over 200.

Remarkably, German production was still at full pressure. Speer, the Minister in charge, has claimed that in 1944 he turned out sufficient tanks to equip 40 Panzer Divisions. Half-track production reached 7,800 that year and Panthers, now much improved in reliability, were appearing at a rate of 330 a month. All this, despite the fact that Allied air action was accounting for 30% of production. It was not equipment that the Army needed but trained soldiers and trained tank crews in particular. By May 1945 the entire armoured force had disintegrated, most of it crushed under the Russian steamroller.

CONCLUSIONS

The story of German armour is a remarkable one. Years of study by dedicated professionals, superb leadership on the battlefield, sound training and high tactical skill, combined with a forceful and imaginative equipment policy, had produced some notable achievements. Good though their equipment was, it was above all the Germans' ability to achieve surprise, their great flexibility, enabling them to produce numerical superiority at the "Schwerpunkt", and the fighting spirit and determination of their soldiers, which were the telling factors in many of their successes. Balanced forces, exceptional skill and understanding in the handling of anti-tank weapons in attack and defence, and a highly developed system of ground to air communications, also played major parts. On the debit side, the forces of reaction in the High Command, which resolutely refused to grasp the true significance of the rôle of large armoured formations in mobile warfare, combined with Hitler's maniacal insistence upon centralized control and his inability to cease interfering with his field commanders' operations, made ultimate defeat almost inevitable. Having said this of Hitler, one has to acknowledge the part he played in pushing forward the armoured equipment programme, which might have taken a very different form, with priorities quite other than those that Guderian fought so hard to establish. In comparison with the inherent weakness of the High Command system, the shortcomings of the Germans logistics are of lesser significance, though they undoubtedly led to the loss of many opportunities. It is perhaps easy to be overcritical on this score. The difficulties were enormous. The fact that the Army kept going under the conditions it faced in Russia from the outset, and on virtually all fronts from the middle of 1942, was, in itself, a considerable achievement which deserves special study.

It is now well over 25 years since the final defeat of the Third Reich. The nature of warfare has changed out of all recognition, not least because we can no longer expect to have time to build up existing field formations at the outbreak of war. The cost of modern technology seriously inhibits the size of standing armies and the the advent of the tactical nuclear weapon has created considerable confusion of thought. Yet the basic rules governing the successful conduct of tactics at the lower level remain. Despite the risks of training to win a war already fought, we must recognize that there is still much to be learned from the German armoured experience of the years 1919 to 1945.

General Hasso von Manteuffel, commander of 5th Panzer Army. He previously commanded the "Gross Deutschland" Panzer Division.

General Balck, one of the greatest armoured commanders of World War II, whose career included command of 11th Panzer Division, 48 Panzer Corps, 4th Panzer Army (all on the Eastern Front), and Army Group G in the West.

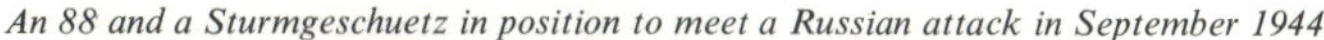

An 88 and a Sturmgeschuetz in position to meet a Russian attack in September 1944.

ORIGINAL PANZER DIVISIONAL SIGNS

1st Panzer

2nd Panzer

3rd Panzer

4th Panzer

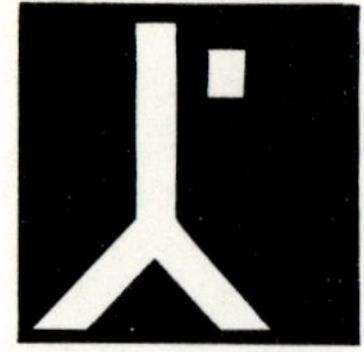
5th Panzer

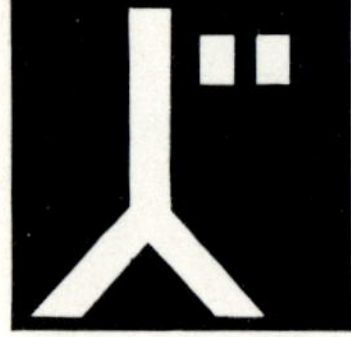
6th Panzer

7th Panzer

8th Panzer

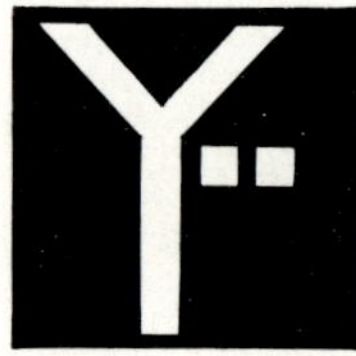
9th Panzer

10th Panzer

PANZER DIVISIONAL SIGNS FROM LATE 1940

After their victory in France in 1940 the Germans doubled the number of their panzer divisions for the next campaign. Signs of the old divisions were changed and the new signs shown here were introduced. Panzer divisions from 21 onwards were formed after 1940. The Gross Deutschland was officially a panzer grenadier division but with its full tank regiment and armoured reconnaissance unit under command it was actually a panzer division.

1st Panzer

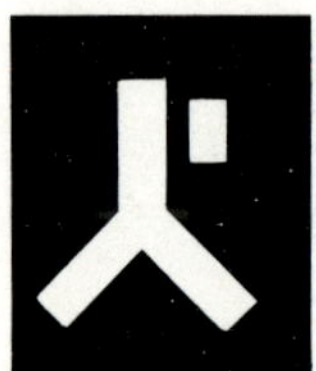
2nd Panzer

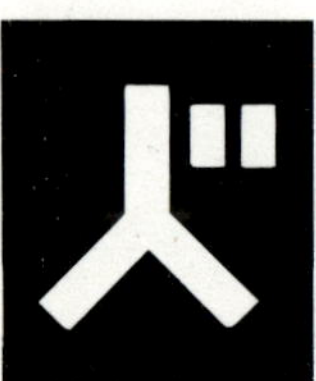
3rd Panzer

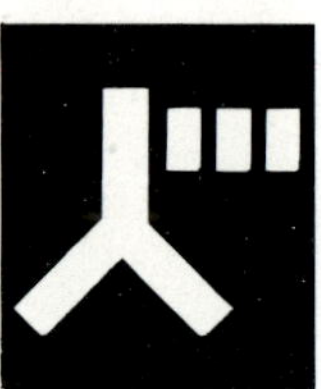
4th Panzer

6th Panzer

5th Panzer

7th Panzer

8th Panzer

9th Panzer

10th Panzer

11th Panzer

12th Panzer

Gross Deutschland

13th Panzer

14th Panzer

15th Panzer

16th Panzer

17th Panzer

18th Panzer

19th Panzer

20th Panzer

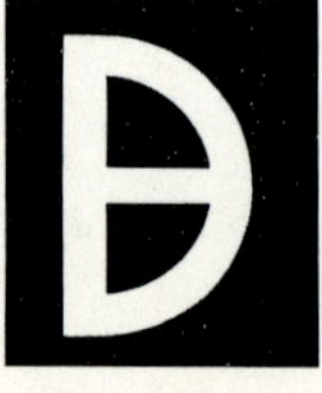
21st Panzer

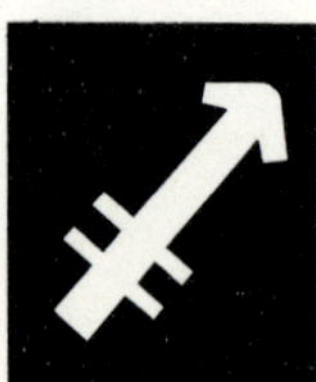
22nd Panzer

23rd Panzer

24th Panzer

25th Panzer

Afrika Korps

116th Panzer

Afrika Korps (variation)

1st Panzer (variation)

4th Panzer (1943)

7th Panzer (1943–44)

19th Panzer (1943–44)

23rd Panzer (variation)

26th Panzer

Panzer Lehr

Kurmark

Feldherrnhalle 2

Hermann Goering

12th Panzer (variation)

SS PANZER DIVISIONAL SIGNS

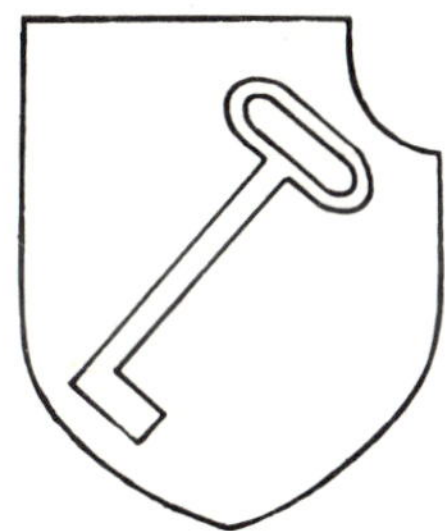
1st SS Panzer Leibstandarte Adolf Hitler

2nd SS Panzer Das Reich

3rd SS Panzer Totenkopf

5th SS Panzer Wiking

9th SS Panzer Hohenstanfen

9th SS Panzer (variation after Arnhem 1944 – red windmill)

10th SS Panzer Frundsberg

12th SS Panzer Hitler Jugend

Achtung Panzer. *Over the hill into battle.*

The Panzer Divisions (1939-1945)

A Short Record of Their Individual Histories Compiled by

DUNCAN CROW *from various authorities*

The first three Panzer Divisions were formed in October 1935.

1st Panzer Division

FORMED in October 1935 at Weimar. Its original establishment was Panzer Brigade 1 (Panzer Regiments 1 and 2, each with two battalions), Motorised Rifle Brigade 1 (Rifle Regiment 1, with two battalions, and Motorcycle Battalion 1), Aufklärung Abteilung 4, Artillerie Regiment 73 (two battalions), and divisional units numbered 37. e.g. Nachrichten Abteilung 37.

The division fought in Poland, September 1939, and in Flanders-France, May-June 1940. In the first part of the latter campaign it attacked Dunkerque.

In October 1940 the division provided Panzer Regiment 2 and cadres for the formation of 16th Panzer Division.

The division fought in Russia, north and centre[1], from the beginning of the campaign in June 1941 until the end of 1942. Early in 1943 it was moved to France, then to the Balkans in June, and in July and August it was in Greece. In November 1943 it returned to Russia (northern Ukraine) and fought in the counter-offensive west of Kiev. In September 1944 it was sent to the Carpathians and took part in the Debrecen counter-attack during the loss of Transylvania. From then until the end of the war the division fought in Hungary and eastern Austria, surrendering in the eastern Austrian Alps area.

Its final full establishment was:

Panzer Aufklärung Abteilung 1
Panzer Regiment 1 (two battalions)
Panzergrenadier Regiment 1 (two battalions)
Panzergrenadier Regiment 113 (two battalions)
Artillerie Regiment 73 (three battalions)
Heeres Flak Abteilung 299
Panzerjaeger Abteilung 37
Nachrichten Abteilung 37
Panzer Pioniere Bataillon 37

Plus divisional HQ, divisional HQ Abteilung, and divisional services.[2]

2nd Panzer Division

Formed in October 1935 at Würzburg. Its original establishment was Panzer Brigade 2 (Panzer Regiments 3 and 4, each with two battalions), Motorised Rifle Brigade 2 (Rifle Regiment 2, with two battalions, and Motorcycle Battalion 2), Aufklärung Abteilung 5, Artillerie Regiment 74 (two battalions), and divisional units numbered 38.

After the Anschluss in March 1938 the division was moved to Vienna. It fought in Poland, September 1939, and then in Flanders-France, May-June 1940. In August 1940 it was moved back to Germany, and in September provided Panzer Regiment 4 and cadres for the formation of 13th Panzer Division.

[1] The German campaign against Russia—Operation Barbarossa—was carried out by Army Groups North, Centre, and South.

[2] Casualties and equipment shortages meant that the actual strengths of Panzer Divisions were rarely up to full establishment—especially was this the case towards the end of World War II.

From September 1940 to February 1941 the division was stationed in Poland. It was then transferred to the Balkans and fought in Greece (April 1941). From Greece it went to France and then, after the opening of the Russian campaign, to Army Group Centre for the drive on Moscow. From the nearby forests it had a brief glimpse of the distant Kremlin.

The division fought in Russia, centre, throughout 1942 and 1943 at Smolensk, Orel, and Kiev. In January 1944 it was moved to Amiens, France, for a re-fit. It fought in Normandy and in the withdrawal across France (June-September 1944), in the Ardennes offensive (December 1944), and in the Rhine battle. It was at Plauen, where it had recently been moved to, when the war ended in May 1945.

Its final full establishment was:

- Panzer Aufklärung Abteilung 2
- Panzer Regiment 3 (two battalions)
- Panzergrenadier Regiment 2 (two battalions)
- Panzergrenadier Regiment 304 (two battalions)
- Artillerie Regiment 74 (three battalions)
- Heeres Flak Abteilung 273
- Panzerjaeger Abteilung 38
- Nachrichten Abteilung 38
- Panzer Pioniere Bataillon 38

Plus divisional HQ, divisional HQ Abteilung, and divisional services.

3rd Panzer Division

Formed in October 1935 in Berlin. Its original establishment was Panzer Brigade 3 "Berlin" (Panzer Regiments 5 "Wünsdorf" and 6 "Neuruppin", each with two battalions), Motorised Rifle Brigade 3 "Eberswalde" (Rifle Regiment 3 "Eberswalde", with two battalions, and Motorcycle Battalion 3 "Freienwalde"), Aufklärung Abteilung 3, Artillerie Regiment 75 "Eberswalde" (two battalions), and divisional units numbered 39.

The division fought in Poland, September 1939, and in Flanders-France, May-June 1940. It then returned to

Panzer IV, Ausf.C, of 2nd Panzer Division.

Germany and provided Panzer Regiment 5 and cadres for the formation of 5th Light Motorised (later 21st Panzer) Division.

From the beginning of the Russian campaign in June 1941 until February 1942 the division fought in Russia, centre, and was then transferred to the south. In the summer of 1943 it was heavily engaged in the Kharkov area and in September moved to the Dnepr bend. Throughout 1944 the division fought in the Ukraine and in Poland. In January 1945 it was moved to Hungary where it fought until April when it was transferred to Austria. It surrendered to the Americans in Styria.

Its final full establishment was:

- Panzer Aufklärung Abteilung 3
- Panzer Regiment 6 (two battalions)
- Panzergrenadier Regiment 3 (two battalions)
- Panzergrenadier Regiment 394 (two battalions)
- Artillerie Regiment 75 (three battalions)
- Heeres Flak Abteilung 314
- Panzerjaeger Abteilung 39
- Nachrichten Abteilung 39
- Panzer Pioniere Bataillon 39

Plus divisional HQ, divisional HQ Abteilung, and divisional services.

A motorised column passing a Panzer II on a road in southern Norway, April 1940. No Panzer divisions were sent to Norway, but individual tank units played a significant part in the campaign.

StuG III caught in the toils of a Russian winter. Self-propelled artillery was an important element in the Panzer Division. (Axel Duckert)

The next two Panzer Divisions, the 4th and 5th, were formed in 1938. Another, the 10th, was formed early in 1939. Six Panzer Divisions, the 1st to 5th inclusive and the 10th, were thus formed before the beginning of World War II on September 1, 1939. All six took part in the Polish campaign of September 1939.

4th Panzer Division

Formed in 1938 at Würzburg. Its original establishment was Panzer Brigade 7 (Panzer Regiments 35 and 36, each with two battalions), Motorised Rifle Brigade 4 (Rifle Regiments 12 and 33, each with two battalions, and Motorcycle Battalion 4), Aufklärung Abteilung 7, Artillerie Regiment 103, and divisional units numbered 84.

The division fought in Poland, September 1939, and in Flanders-France, May-June 1940. In October 1940 the division provided Panzer Regiment 36 and cadres for the formation of 14th Panzer Division.

From the beginning of the Russian campaign in June 1941 the division fought continuously in Russia, centre. It took part in the northern pincer of the Kursk offensive in July 1943, and when this failed played an important part in the defensive fighting in the Gomel area. When the Russian advances began again in the summer of 1944 the division fell back towards Latvia. Early in 1945 it moved into Germany where its remnants later surrendered to the Americans.

Its final full establishment was:

Panzer Aufklärung Abteilung 4
Panzer Regiment 35 (two battalions)
Panzergrenadier Regiment 12 (two battalions)
Panzergrenadier Regiment 33 (two battalions)
Artillerie Regiment 103 (three battalions)
Heeres Flak Abteilung 290
Panzerjaeger Abteilung 49
Nachrichten Abteilung 79
Panzer Pioniere Bataillon 79

Plus divisional HQ, divisional HQ Abteilung, and divisional services.

5th Panzer Division

Formed in November 1938 at Oppeln. Its original establishment was Panzer Brigade 8 (Panzer Regiments 15 and 31, each with two battalions), Motorised Rifle Brigade 5 (Rifle Regiments 13 and 14, each with two battalions, and Motorcycle Battalion 5), Aufklärung Abteilung 8, Artillerie Regiment 116 (two battalions), Panzer Abwehr Abteilung 53 (from March 1940, Panzerjaeger Abteilung 53), Nachrichten Abteilung 77, and Panzer Pioniere Bataillon 89.

The division fought in Poland, September 1939, and then in Flanders-France, May-June 1940. In October 1940 it provided Panzer Regiment 15 and cadres for the formation of 11th Panzer Division.

The division fought in the Balkans, driving north from Bulgaria to Nis in Jugoslavia and then fighting in Greece in April 1941. In June 1941 it fought in Russia, centre, from the opening of the campaign, first in the drive on Moscow and then in the Rzhev-Gzhatsk area to the west of the capital. The division fought at Orel during the Battle of Kursk and suffered heavily. Early in 1944 it fought in the area west of the middle Dnepr. Later in the year it moved back into Latvia and Kurland.

At the beginning of 1945, before the opening of the Russian offensive, the division was in East Prussia. It finally surrendered to the Russians after a fierce defence of the Hela peninsula north of Danzig.

Its final establishment was:

Panzer Aufklärung Abteilung 5
Panzer Regiment 31 (two battalions)
Panzergrenadier Regiment 13 (two battalions)
Panzergrenadier Regiment 14 (two battalions)
Artillerie Regiment 116 (three battalions)
Heeres Flak Abteilung 228
Panzerjaeger Abteilung 53
Nachrichten Abteilung 77
Panzer Pioniere Bataillon 89

Plus divisional HQ, divisional HQ Abteilung, and divisional services.

After the Polish campaign four more Panzer Divisions (the 6th, 7th, 8th, and 9th) were formed by the conversion of the four Light Divisions which had all fought in Poland.

6th Panzer Division

Formed in October 1939 at Wuppertal from the 1st Light Division with three tank battalions (Panzer Regiment 11, with two battalions, and Panzer Abteilung 65), Rifle Brigade 6 (Rifle Regiment 4, with three battalions, and Motorcycle Battalion 6), Aufklärung Abteilung 57, Artillerie Regiment 76 (two battalions), and divisional units numbered 57, except Panzer Abwehr Abteilung 41 (from March 1940, Panzerjaeger Abteilung 41) and Nachrichten Abteilung 82.

The division fought in Flanders and France, May-June 1940, and was then posted to East Prussia. From June 1941 it fought in Russia, first in the Leningrad area and then in the central part of the front where it suffered heavy losses, to the extent that for some weeks it fought on foot because it had lost every single vehicle and at one time was reduced almost to company strength.

In May 1942 the remnants of the division were moved to France for rest and re-fitting. In December it returned to Russia, this time to the south, taking part in Fourth Panzer Army's attempt to break through to 6th Army in Stalingrad, and was then engaged in the Kharkov area until July 1943 when it took part in the Belgorod offensive (the southern pincer of the Battle of Kursk). In January 1944 it moved to Hungary and later fought in the defence of Budapest. In March 1945 it withdrew into Austria and surrendered to the Russians at Brno in Czechoslovakia in May.

Motor-cycle troops of 6th Panzer Division. In the background three Panzer 35(t).

Its final full establishment was:

Panzer Aufklärung Abteilung 6
Panzer Regiment 11 (two battalions)
Panzergrenadier Regiment 4 (two battalions)
Panzergrenadier Regiment 114 (two battalions)
Artillerie Regiment 76 (three battalions)
Heeres Flak Abteilung 298
Panzerjaeger Abteilung 41
Nachrichten Abteilung 82
Panzer Pioniere Bataillon 57

Plus divisional HQ, divisional HQ Abteilung, and divisional services.

7th Panzer Division

Formed in October 1939 with three tank battalions (Panzer Regiment 25, with two battalions, and Panzer Abteilung 66), Rifle Brigade 7 (Rifle Regiments 6 and 7, each with two battalions, and Motorcycle Battalion 7), Aufklärung Abteilung 58, Artillerie Regiment 78 (two battalions), and divisional units numbered 58, except Panzer Abwehr Abteilung 42 (from March 1940, Panzerjaeger Abteilung 42) and Nachrichten Abteilung 83.

The division fought in Flanders and France, May-June 1940. In February 1941 it returned to Germany and in

7th Panzer Division halted during its sweep across northern France to Cherbourg in June 1940. The division at this time was commanded by General Erwin Rommel. The tank on the extreme left is a Panzer 38(t).

Tanks of 8th Panzer Division negotiating a water hazard, Russia, 1941. Panzer IIs in the background.

July was sent to Russia, centre. It fought in Russia until June 1942 when it was sent back to France and took part in the occupation of the southern part of the country in November.

In December 1942 the division returned to Russia, this time to the south, and fought in the Belgorod offensive (the southern pincer of the Battle of Kursk), and at Kharkov in August 1943. In August 1944 it was moved to the Baltic States and fought in Kurland and at Memel until November. When the Russian offensive was renewed it gradually withdrew to the west, surrendering to British troops at Schwerin in May 1945.

Its final full establishment was:

Panzer Aufklärung Abteilung 7
Panzer Regiment 25 (two battalions)
Panzergrenadier Regiment 6 (two battalions)
Panzergrenadier Regiment 7 (two battalions)
Artillerie Regiment 78 (three battalions)
Heeres Flak Abteilung 296
Panzerjaeger Abteilung 42
Nachrichten Abteilung 83
Panzer Pioniere Bataillon 58

Plus divisional HQ, divisional HQ Abteilung, and divisional services.

8th Panzer Division

Formed in October 1939 from the 3rd Light Division with three tank battalions (Panzer Regiment 10, with two battalions, and Panzer Abteilung 67), Rifle Brigade 8 (Rifle Regiment 8, with three battalions, and Motorcycle Battalion 8), Aufklärung Abteilung 59, Artillerie Regiment 80 (two battalions), and divisional units numbered 59, except Panzer Abwehr Abteilung 43 (from March 1940, Panzerjaeger Abteilung 43) and Nachrichten Abteilung 84.

The division fought in Flanders and France, May-June 1940. In April 1941 it motored into northern Jugoslavia to Zagreb. In July it went to Russia, north, taking part in the beginning of the siege of Leningrad. From March to November 1942 it fought at Cholm. From April to August 1943 it was engaged in the Orel area, taking part in the northern pincer of the Battle of Kursk and the subsequent withdrawal in face of the Russian counter-offensive. In October it suffered severely in the withdrawal from Kiev. Until September 1944 it fought in Russia, south, then moved to the Carpathian Mountains and from there to the defence of Budapest. The division withdrew into Moravia and surrendered to the Russians at Brno in May 1945.

Its final full establishment was:

Panzer Aufklärung Abteilung 8
Panzer Regiment 10 (one battalion)
Panzergrenadier Regiment 8 (two battalions)
Panzergrenadier Regiment 28 (two battalions)
Artillerie Regiment 80 (three battalions)
Heeres Flak Abteilung 286
Panzerjaeger Abteilung 42
Nachrichten Abteilung 84
Panzer Pioniere Bataillon 59

Plus divisional HQ, divisional HQ Abteilung, and divisional services.

9th Panzer Division

Formed in January 1940 from the 4th Light Division with Panzer Regiment 33 (two battalions), Rifle Brigade 9 (Rifle Regiments 10 and 11, each with two battalions,

After being badly battered in Russia the remnants of 9th Panzer Division were moved to the south of France to be re-formed.

and Motorcycle Battalion 59), Aufklärung Abteilung 9, Artillerie Regiment 102 (two battalions), and divisional units numbered 60, except Panzer Abwehr Abteilung 50 (from March 1940, Panzerjaeger Abteilung 50), Nachrichten Abteilung 85, and Pioniere Bataillon 86. In parenthesis it may be noted that Panzer Regiment 33 was composed of members of the former Austrian Army tank battalion that, after the Anschluss in 1938, was incorporated into the German Wehrmacht as Panzer Abteilung 33. In March 1943 Panzer Regiment 33 was officially given the name Prinz Eugen Panzer Regiment.

In May 1940 the 9th fought in Holland, the only panzer division to do so. From Breda (Holland) it drove south to Antwerp, Brussels and Mons, and then to Arras, from where it went north to Dunkerque. In the second part of the campaign it had a hard time near Amiens and then thrust south to Lyons.

From September to December 1940 the division was in Poland and was then sent to the Balkans. On April 6, 1941 it struck south-west from the western frontier of Bulgaria towards Skopje in Jugoslavia.

After the Balkans campaign the division was sent to Russia, south, in July, and in October was moved to Russia, centre. It took part in the Battle of Kursk and was then closely committed in the Dnepr bend. After being badly cut up in Russia, south, the remnants of the division in March 1944 were moved to the Nîmes area in the south of France where they were combined with the 155th Reserve Panzer Division to re-form the 9th Panzer Division.

The division fought in the Normandy and Falaise battles, and in September 1944 was fighting in the Aachen area. In December it took part in the Ardennes offensive. The division was surrounded in the Ruhr and captured in the "Ruhr Pocket" in April 1945.

Its final full establishment was:

Panzer Aufklärung Abteilung 9
Panzer Regiment 33 (one battalion)
Panzer Abteilung 51 (from March 1, 1944)
Panzergrenadier Regiment 10 (two battalions)
Panzergrenadier Regiment 11 (two battalions)
Artillerie Regiment 102 (three battalions)
Heeres Flak Abteilung 287
Panzerjaeger Abteilung 50
Nachrichten Abteilung 85
Panzer Pioniere Bataillon 86

Plus divisional HQ, divisional HQ Abteilung, and divisional services.

10th Panzer Division

Formed in April 1939 in Prague with Panzer Brigade 4 (Panzer Regiments 7 and 8, each with two battalions), Rifle Brigade 10 (Rifle Regiments 69 and 86, each with two battalions), Aufklärung Abteilung 90, Artillerie Regiment (two battalions) and other divisional units numbered 90, except Pioniere Bataillon 49.

The division fought in Poland in 1939 and then in the Flanders-France campaign in May-June 1940. In the first part of the campaign it captured Calais.

Later in 1940 it provided Panzer Regiment 8 and cadres for the new 15th Panzer Division.

In July 1941 the division went to Russia, centre, until April 1942, when it was sent to France for re-fitting. It repulsed the Canadian armoured raid on Dieppe on August 19, 1942.

In December 1942 the division was sent to Tunisia,

Panzer IV, Ausf.B, moving along a flooded road in Belgium, May 1940. Ten Panzer Divisions took part in the campaign in the West against France.

where it was destroyed in May 1943 and never re-formed.

Its final full establishment was:

- Panzer Aufklärung Abteilung 10
- Panzer Regiment 7 (two battalions)
- Panzergrenadier Brigade 10 (Panzergrenadier Regiments 69 and 86, each with two battalions)
- Artillerie Regiment 90 (three battalions)
- Heeres Flak Abteilung 302*
- Panzerjaeger Abteilung 90
- Nachrichten Abteilung 90
- Panzer Pioniere Bataillon 49

The next ten Panzer Divisions, the 11th to 20th inclusive, were all formed in August or October 1940, as was an eleventh, the 23rd.

11th Panzer Division

Formed in August 1940 from the 11th Rifle Brigade with the 15th Panzer Regiment and cadres from the 5th Panzer Division. Its original establishment was Panzer Regiment 15 (two battalions), Rifle Brigade 11 (Rifle Regiments 110 and 111, each with two battalions, and Motorcycle Battalion 61), Aufklärung Abteilung 231, Artillerie Regiment 119 (three battalions), Nachrichten Abteilung 341, Pioniere Abteilung 209, and other divisional units numbered 61.

The division took part in the Balkan campaign from January to April 1941, driving north from Bulgaria through Nis to Belgrade and being credited with the capture of the Jugoslav capital on April 12.

Among the foreign tanks taken into German service were two Czech types: the TNHP (seen on the extreme left of the 7th Panzer Division picture), and the LTM–35 (seen here in Russia). The TNHP was designated Panzer 38(t) by the Germans, and the LTM–35 was designated Panzer 35(t). (t) =tschechisch =Czechoslovakian.

In July 1941 the division went to Russia, fighting first in the south, then in the centre until June 1942, then in the south again. It took part in the Belgorod offensive (the southern German pincer in the Battle of Kursk) in July 1943, and was then heavily engaged in the Krivoy Rog area in the Dnepr bend. Early in 1944 the division suffered severely in the Korsun encirclement south of Kiev and in June its remnants were sent to France for rest and re-fit.

The division next fought in southern France against the advancing United States Seventh and French First Armies after the Riviera landings in August 1944. It withdrew to Alsace, defended the Belfort Gap in September, and then moved north to the Saar. It fought at Remagen in March 1945 and, at the end of the war, surrendered to the Americans in Bavaria.

Its final full establishment was:

- Panzer Aufklärung Abteilung 11
- Panzer Regiment 15 (three battalions)
- Panzergrenadier Regiment 110 (two battalions)
- Panzergrenadier Regiment 111 (two battalions)
- Artillerie Regiment 119 (three battalions)
- Heeres Flak Abteilung 277
- Panzerjaeger Abteilung 61
- Nachrichten Abteilung 89
- Panzer Pioniere Bataillon 209

Plus divisional HQ, divisional HQ Abteilung, and divisional services. The 11th was known as the Gespenst [Ghost] Division.

12th Panzer Division

Formed in October 1940 in Germany from the 2nd Infantry Division (Motorised) with Panzer Regiment 29 (three battalions), Rifle Brigade 12 (Rifle Regiments 5 and 25, and Motorcycle Battalion 22), Aufklärung Abteilung 2, Artillerie Regiment (three battalions) and other divisional units numbered 2, except Pioniere Battalion 32.

The division fought in Russia, centre, from July 1941; then moved in September to Army Group North where it took part in the siege of Leningrad until November 1942 when it moved back to Army Group Centre. From March to August 1943 it was on the Orel front and subsequently took part in the defence of the middle Dnepr. In February 1944 the division returned to the north and in August retired to Kurland where it was captured by the Russians in 1945.

Its final full establishment was:

- Panzer Aufklärung Abteilung 12
- Panzer Regiment 29 (two battalions)
- Panzergrenadier Regiment 5 (two battalions)
- Panzergrenadier Regiment 25 (two battalions)
- Artillerie Regiment 2 (three battalions)
- Heeres Flak Abteilung 303
- Panzerjaeger Abteilung 2
- Nachrichten Abteilung 2
- Panzer Pioniere Bataillon 32

Plus divisional HQ, divisional HQ Abteilung, and divisional services.

13th Panzer Division

Formed in October 1940 in Rumania where it served as a training unit until June 1941. Its original establishment was Panzer Regiment 4 (two battalions) from 2nd Panzer Division, Rifle Brigade 13 (Rifle Regiments 66 and 93, each with two battalions, and Motorcycle Battalion 43), Aufklärung Abteilung 13, Artillerie Regiment (three battalions) and other divisional units numbered 13, except Pioniere Bataillon 4.

In June 1941 the division moved from Rumania to Russia, south, where it took part in the capture of Kiev. From October 1942 to January 1943 it was in the Caucasus, and from February to August in the Kuban. From October 1943 to January 1944 the division fought around Krivoy Rog in the Dnepr bend.

At this period the division's establishment was:

Panzer Aufklärung Abteilung 13
Panzer Regiment 4 (two battalions)
Panzergrenadier Regiment 66 (two battalions)
Panzergrenadier Regiment 93 (two battalions)
Artillerie Regiment 13 (three battalions)
Heeres Flak Abteilung 271
Panzerjaeger Abteilung 13
Nachrichten Abteilung 13
Panzer Pioniere Bataillon 4

Plus divisional HQ, divisional HQ Abteilung, and divisional services.

In May 1944 Panzergrenadier Regiment 1030 "Feldherrnhalle" was added to the division but was destroyed in the southern Ukraine soon afterwards. The division itself retired to Germany for re-fitting in September and in October was sent to Hungary. In January 1945 it was destroyed in the defence of Budapest but was immediately re-constituted as Panzer Division "Feldherrnhalle 2".

Panzer Division Feldherrnhalle 2

Formed at the beginning of 1945 with elements of the destroyed 13th Panzer Division and the destroyed Panzergrenadier Division 60 "Feldherrnhalle", both of which were decimated in the fighting at Budapest. From

Another foreign tank taken into German service was the French Hotchkiss H39. This particular tank, with German modifications, is preserved in the Établishment du Matériel de Gien. (Collection Pitaud).

Hungary the division fought its way back to Austria where it was at the end of the war.

Its final establishment was:

Panzer Aufklärung Abteilung Feldherrnhalle 2
Panzer Regiment Feldherrnhalle 2
Panzergrenadier Regiment Feldherrnhalle 2
Panzerfüsilier Regiment Feldherrnhalle 2
Panzer Artillerie Regiment Feldherrnhalle 2
Panzer Sturmgeschütz Brigade Feldherrnhalle 2
Heeres Flak Abteilung Feldherrnhalle 2
Panzerjaeger Abteilung Feldherrnhalle 2
Nachrichten Abteilung Feldherrnhalle 2
Panzer Pioniere Bataillon Feldherrnhalle 2

14th Panzer Division

Formed in August 1940 from the 4th Infantry Division with Panzer Regiment 36 (two battalions) from 4th Panzer Division, Rifle Brigade 14 (Rifle Regiments 103 and 108, each with two battalions, and Motorcycle Battalion 64), Aufklärung Abteilung 4, Artillerie Regiment (three battalions) and other divisional units numbered 4, except Nachrichten Abteilung 40 and Pioniere Bataillon 13.

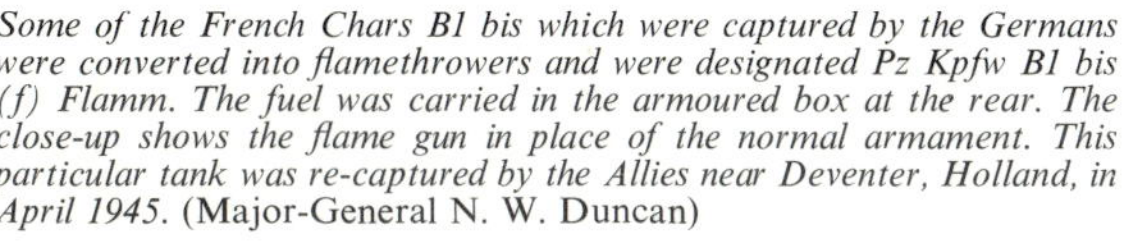

Some of the French Chars B1 bis which were captured by the Germans were converted into flamethrowers and were designated Pz Kpfw B1 bis (f) Flamm. The fuel was carried in the armoured box at the rear. The close-up shows the flame gun in place of the normal armament. This particular tank was re-captured by the Allies near Deventer, Holland, in April 1945. (Major-General N. W. Duncan)

In March 1941 the division was transferred from Germany to Hungary to take part in the Balkans campaign. In April it motored into northern Jugoslavia heading for Belgrade. In May and June it was in Germany re-fitting for the Russian campaign.

From July 1941 to December 1942 the division fought in Russia, south, and was surrounded and destroyed at Stalingrad with 6th Army and Panzer Divisions 16 and 24.

The division was re-formed in Brittany, April-October 1943, and was then sent to Russia in November to the Dnepr bend. It was re-fitted in the Ukraine in June 1944, moved to Kurland in August, and was captured there by the Russians in April 1945.

Its final full establishment was:

Panzer Aufklärung Abteilung 14
Panzer Regiment 36 (three battalions)
Panzergrenadier Regiment 103 (two battalions)
Panzergrenadier Regiment 108 (two battalions)
Artillerie Regiment 4 (three battalions)
Heeres Flak Abteilung 276
Panzerjaeger Abteilung 4
Nachrichten Abteilung 4
Panzer Pioniere Bataillon 13

Plus divisional HQ, divisional HQ Abteilung, and divisional services.

15th Panzer Division

Formed in August 1940 from the 33rd Infantry Division with Panzer Regiment 8 (two battalions) from 10th Panzer Division, Rifle Regiments 104 and 115, each with two battalions, Motorcycle Battalion 15, Aufklärung Abteilung 115, Artillerie Regiment (three battalions) and other divisional units numbered 33.

In April 1941 the division went to Libya as part of Afrikakorps and fought throughout the rest of the campaign along the North African littoral, surrendering with the rest of the Axis forces in Tunisia on May 12, 1943.

Its final full establishment was:

Panzer Aufklärung Abteilung 15[1]
Panzer Regiment 8 (two battalions)
Panzergrenadier Regiment 104 (two battalions)
Panzergrenadier Regiment 115 (two battalions)
Artillerie Regiment 33 (three battalions)
Heeres Flak Abteilung 315
Panzerjaeger Abteilung 33
Nachrichten Abteilung 33
Panzer Pioniere Bataillon 33

Plus divisional HQ, divisional HQ Abteilung, and divisional services.

In July 1943 in Sicily it was re-formed as the 15th Panzergrenadier Division.

16th Panzer Division

Formed in August 1940 with Panzer Regiment 2 (two battalions) from 1st Panzer Division, Rifle Brigade 16 (Rifle Regiments 64 and 79, each with two battalions, and Motorcycle Battalion 16), Aufklärung Abteilung 16, Artillerie Regiment (three battalions) and other divisional units numbered 16.

After being held in reserve during the Balkans campaign the division was sent to Russia, south, where it was continuously engaged until its encirclement and destruction at Stalingrad with 6th Army and Panzer Divisions 14 and 24.

The division was re-formed in France in March 1943. During the negotiations which culminated in Italy leaving the Axis and capitulating to the Allies it was sent to northern Italy and then to Taranto. In September it was moved hastily to Salerno just before the Allied landings and had hard fighting both there and in the Naples area.

In November 1943 the division returned to Russia to take part in the German offensive west of Kiev. It suffered heavy losses and withdrew to the Baranow area (on the River Vistula north-east of Cracow). In October 1944 it was re-fitted at Kielce and in January 1945 took part in the fighting against the Russian attack from the Baranow bridgehead. In April it had withdrawn to Brno in Czechoslovakia where part of the division surrendered to the Russians and part to the Americans.

Its final full establishment was:

Panzer Aufklärung Abteilung 16
Panzer Regiment 2 (two battalions)
Panzergrenadier Regiment 64 (two battalions)
Panzergrenadier Regiment 79 (two battalions)
Panzer Artillerie Regiment 16 (three battalions)
Heeres Flak Abteilung 274
Panzerjaeger Abteilung 4
Nachrichten Abteilung 16
Panzer Pioniere Bataillon 16

Plus divisional HQ, divisional HQ Abteilung, and divisional services.

17th Panzer Division

Formed in October 1940 with Panzer Regiment 17 (two battalions), Rifle Brigade 17 (Rifle Regiments 40 and 63, each with two battalions, and Motorcycle Battalion 17), Aufklärung Abteilung 17, Artillerie Regiment (three battalions) and other divisional units numbered 27.

The division fought in Russia, centre, from June 1941 to November 1942, and then in the south where it took part in Fourth Panzer Army's attempt to relieve 6th Army in Stalingrad. In summer 1943 it was in the Donets and Dnepr bend sectors. From March 1944 it was in the withdrawal across northern Ukraine. In January 1945 it was fighting in the Baranow bridgehead area. In April it was overrun by the Russians.

Its final full establishment was:

Panzer Aufklärung Abteilung 17
Panzer Regiment 17 (two battalions)
Panzergrenadier Regiment 40 (two battalions)
Panzergrenadier Regiment 63 (two battalions)
Panzer Artillerie Regiment 27 (three battalions)
Heeres Flak Abteilung 297
Panzerjaeger Abteilung 27
Nachrichten Abteilung 27
Panzer Pioniere Bataillon 27

Plus divisional HQ, divisional HQ Abteilung, and divisional services.

18th Panzer Division

Formed in October 1940 with Panzer Regiment 18 (two battalions), Rifle Brigade 18 (Rifle Regiments 52 and 101, each with two battalions, and Motorcycle Battalion 18), Aufklärung Abteilung 18, Artillerie

[1] In his *Panzer Battles 1939–1945* Major-General F. W. Von Mellenthin refers to this unit throughout the Libyan campaign as 33rd Recce.

StuG III driving into the blazing waste of a Russian town.

Regiment (three battalions) and other divisional units numbered 88.

The division fought in Russia, centre, from June 1941 to June 1942, then in the south, then in the centre again. In October and November 1943 it was in action west of Kiev, where it suffered heavily in the German counter-offensive. In consequence of its losses it was re-organised as the 18th Artillery Division.

Its final full establishment as a panzer division was:

- Panzer Aufklärung Abteilung 18
- Panzer Regiment 18 (two battalions)
- Panzergrenadier Regiment 52 (two battalions)
- Panzergrenadier Regiment 101 (two battalions)
- Panzer Artillerie Regiment 88 (three battalions)
- Heeres Flak Abteilung 280
- Panzerjaeger Abteilung 88
- Nachrichten Abteilung 88
- Panzer Pioniere Bataillon 88

Plus divisional HQ, divisional HQ Abteilung, and divisional services.

19th Panzer Division

Formed in October 1940 with Panzer Regiment 27 (two battalions), Rifle Brigade 19 (Rifle Regiments 73 and 74, each with two battalions, and Motorcycle Battalion 19), Aufklärung Abteilung 19, Artillerie Regiment (three battalions) and other divisional units numbered 19.

The division fought in Russia, centre, from June 1941 to April 1943, when it was transferred to the south. In July 1943 it was in the Belgorod offensive (the southern pincer of the Battle of Kursk) where it suffered heavy losses. In March 1944 it was in the withdrawal across northern Ukraine. From July until the end of the year it was in East Prussia and was then moved to Radom, south of Warsaw. In January and February 1945 it fought against the Russian break-out from the Baranow bridgehead, withdrawing towards Breslau. In February it moved south to Silezice in Bohemia and was there when the war ended.

Its final full establishment was:

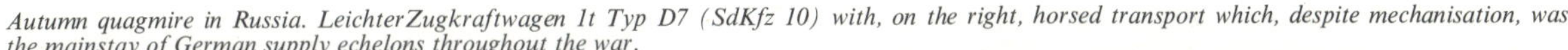

Autumn quagmire in Russia. LeichterZugkraftwagen 1t Typ D7 (SdKfz 10) with, on the right, horsed transport which, despite mechanisation, was the mainstay of German supply echelons throughout the war.

Panzer Aufklärung Abteilung 19
Panzer Regiment 27 (two battalions)
Panzergrenadier Regiment 73 (two battalions)
Panzergrenadier Regiment 74 (two battalions)
Panzer Artillerie Regiment 19 (three battalions)
Heeres Flak Abteilung 272
Panzerjaeger Abteilung 19
Nachrichten Abteilung 19
Panzer Pioniere Bataillon 19

Plus divisional HQ, divisional HQ Abteilung, and divisional services.

20th Panzer Division

Formed in October 1940 with Panzer Regiment 21 (two battalions), Rifle Brigade 20 (Rifle Regiments 59 and 112, each with two battalions, and Motorcycle Battalion 20), Aufklärung Abteilung 92, Artillerie Regiment (three battalions) and other divisional units numbered 92.

The division fought in Russia, centre, from the beginning of the campaign, taking part in the initial drive on Moscow and continuing to be engaged thereafter. In July 1943 it was in the Orel offensive (the northern pincer of the Battle of Kursk). In the summer of 1944 it fought against the Russian offensive, suffered heavily, was transferred to Rumania in August, and was there engaged in fierce fighting. In November 1944 it was moved to East Prussia, and then in December it was moved south to Hungary. The division was overrun in May 1945 in the central sector of the Eastern front.

Its final full establishment was:

Panzer Aufklärung Abteilung 20
Panzer Regiment 21 (two battalions)
Panzergrenadier Regiment 59 (two battalions)
Panzergrenadier Regiment 112 (two battalions)
Panzer Artillerie Regiment 92 (three battalions)
Panzerjaeger Abteilung 92
Nachrichten Abteilung 92
Panzer Pioniere Bataillon 92

Plus divisional HQ, divisional HQ Abteilung, and divisional services.

21st Panzer Division

Formed in February 1941 from 5th Light Motorised Division with Panzer Regiment 5 and cadres from 3rd Panzer Division.

The division went to Libya as part of Afrikakorps in February 1941 and fought throughout the rest of the campaign along the North African littoral. After the Second Battle of El Alamein in October-November 1942 the division, having taken part in the battle, provided the rear-guard during the withdrawal to Tripoli and Tunisia. It surrendered with the rest of the Axis troops in Tunisia in May 1943.

Its final establishment was:

Panzer Regiment 22 (two battalions)
Rifle Regiment 125 (two battalions)
Rifle Regiment 192 (two battalions)
Motorcycle Battalion 21
Aufklärung Abteilung 200[1]
Artillerie Regiment 155 (three battalions)
Other divisional units numbered 200, except Pioniere Bataillon 220

---

[1] In his *Panzer Battles 1939–1945* Major-General F. W. Von Mellenthin refers to this unit throughout the Libyan campaign as 3rd Recce.

Panzer III of the Afrikakorps in Tripoli. Like the Desert Rats (the British 7th Armoured Division) the 15th and 21st Panzer Divisions became one of the undying legends of World War II.

Burning oilfields met the German advance into the Caucasus. Leichter Schützenpanzerwagen (SdKfz 250) advance beside a pall of smoke, with their Panzer Grenadier crews.

In July 1943 the division was re-formed in Normandy from occupation troops with the following establishment:

Panzer Aufklärung Abteilung 21
Panzer Regiment 22 (two battalions)
Panzergrenadier Regiment 125 (two battalions)
Panzergrenadier Regiment 192 (two battalions)
Panzer Artillerie Regiment 155 (three battalions)
Panzerjaeger Abteilung 200
Nachrichten Abteilung 200
Panzer Pioniere Bataillon 220

Plus divisional HQ, divisional HQ Abteilung, and divisional services. Heeres Flak Abteilung 305 was added to the division later.

Although scheduled for posting to the Eastern front the division's orders were cancelled and it remained in France where it fought against the Allied landings in Normandy in June 1944 and was engaged in the subsequent withdrawal from France. After re-fitting in Germany it returned to the Western front from September to December in the Saar and northern Alsace. In January 1945 it finally moved to the Eastern front, centre, where it was overrun by the Russians at the end of the war.

22nd Panzer Division

Formed in 1941. The division was sent to Russia, south, in March 1942 and fought in the Crimea. It then fought in the Don bend near Stalingrad and was almost destroyed there in November 1942 when the Russian offensive began.

Its final full establishment was:

Panzer Aufklärung Abteilung 140
Panzer Regiment 204 (two battalions)
Panzergrenadier Regiment 129 (two battalions)
Panzergrenadier Regiment 140 (two battalions)
Panzer Artillerie Regiment (three battalions)
Heeres Flak Abteilung 289
Panzerjaeger Abteilung 140
Nachrichten Abteilung 140
Panzer Pioniere Bataillon 140

Plus divisional HQ, divisional HQ Abteilung, and divisional services.

The division was subsequently disbanded. Panzergrenadier Regiment 129 was posted to 15th Panzergrenadier Division, formerly 15th Panzer Division.

23rd Panzer Division

Formed in October 1940 in France, with Panzer Regiment 23 (two battalions), Rifle Brigade 23 (Rifle Regiments 126 and 128, each with two battalions, and Motorcycle Battalion 23), Aufklärung Abteilung 128, Artillerie Regiment (three battalions) and other divisional units numbered 128.

The division's formation was not completed until October 1941. In March 1942 it was sent to Russia and took part in defeating the Russian offensive against Kharkov in May. In December it took part in Fourth Panzer Army's attempt to break through to 6th Army in Stalingrad. At the end of 1943 it was in the Dnepr bend fighting and suffered severe losses in the withdrawal westwards. It moved to Poland for re-fitting and fought there in September 1944. In October it was moved to Hungary and fought at Debrecen. It then moved north to the Baranow bridgehead and was there when the Russians launched their attack in January 1945. It was overrun by the Russians at the end of the war.

Its final full establishment was:

Panzer Aufklärung Abteilung 23
Panzer Regiment 23 (two battalions)
Panzergrenadier Regiment 126 (two battalions)
Panzergrenadier Regiment 128 (two battalions)
Panzer Artillerie Regiment 128 (three battalions)
Heeres Flak Abteilung 278
Panzerjaeger Abteilung 128
Nachrichten Abteilung 128
Panzer Pioniere Bataillon 128

Plus divisional HQ, divisional HQ Abteilung, and divisional services.

In their retreat from the Caucasus the Germans had to abandon much of their equipment, including these Pz Kpfw IV F2—the first Panzer IVs to be armed with the long-barrelled KwK 40 L/43 7,5cm gun. They were known to the British as "Mark IV Specials".

Stalingrad. Three Panzer Divisions were lost here with Field Marshal Paulus's 6th Army.

24th Panzer Division

Formed in February 1942 from the 1st Cavalry Division, with Panzer Regiment 24 (two battalions), Rifle Brigade 24 (Rifle Regiments 21 and 26, each with two battalions, and Motorcycle Battalion 24), Aufklärung Abteilung 86, Artillerie Regiment 89 (three battalions), and divisional units numbered 40.

The division fought in Russia, where it had previously fought as the 1st Cavalry Division. It was destroyed at Stalingrad in January 1943, re-formed in Normandy in March-April, and sent to Italy in August. In October it returned to Russia, south, where it suffered heavily west of Kiev in November.

The division suffered heavily again in March 1944 during the general withdrawal from the Dnepr bend. In July it was in southern Poland, and in October it was in Hungary where it took part in the Debrecen counter-attack. From December 1944 to January 1945 it was in Slovakia from where it was sent to west Prussia. It withdrew into Schleswig-Holstein where it surrendered to the British in May 1945.

Its final full establishment was:

Panzer Aufklärung Abteilung 24
Panzer Regiment 24 (two battalions)
Panzergrenadier Regiment 21 (two battalions)
Panzergrenadier Regiment 26 (two battalions)
Panzer Artillerie Regiment 89 (three battalions)
Heeres Flak Abteilung 283
Panzerjaeger Abteilung 40
Nachrichten Abteilung 86
Panzer Pioniere Bataillon 40

Plus divisional HQ, divisional HQ Abteilung, and divisional services.

25th Panzer Division

Formed in February 1942 from occupation troops in Norway. It was moved to southern France in August

1943 and then to Russia, south, in October. This latter move was against the advice of the Inspector-General of Armoured Troops (Colonel-General Guderian) who considered that the division was not yet ready for action. "This unfortunate division," as Guderian called it in his memoirs, was committed to action near Kiev in November. It suffered heavy losses in the withdrawal across northern Ukraine in March 1944, and in April it was sent to Denmark to be re-formed.

In September 1944 the division returned to the Eastern front, this time to the central sector, where it fought in the Vistula area. Throughout January 1945 it was engaged in the defence of Warsaw, and it then withdrew into Germany where it was over-run by the Russians in May.

Its final full establishment was:

Panzer Aufklärung Abteilung 87
Panzer Regiment 9 (two battalions)
Panzergrenadier Regiment 146 (two battalions)
Panzergrenadier Regiment 147 (two battalions)
Panzer Artillerie Regiment 91 (three battalions)
Heeres Flak Abteilung 284
Panzerjaeger Abteilung 87
Nachrichten Abteilung 87
Panzer Pioniere Bataillon 87

Plus divisional HQ, divisional HQ Abteilung, and divisional services.

26th Panzer Division

Formed in October 1942 in Brittany by the conversion of the 23rd Infantry Division, with Panzer Regiment 26 (two battalions), Rifle Brigade 26 (Rifle Regiments 9 and 67, each with two battalions, and Motorcycle Battalion 26), Aufklärung Abteilung 26, Artillerie Regiment (three battalions) and other divisional units numbered 93.

The division was sent to Italy after the fall of Mussolini in July 1943 and fought there until the end of the war, surrendering near Bologna in May 1945.

Its final full establishment was:

Panzer Aufklärung Abteilung 26
Panzer Regiment 26 (two battalions)
Panzergrenadier Regiment 9 (two battalions)
Panzergrenadier Regiment 67 (two battalions)
Verstärktes Grenadier Regiment (two battalions)[1]
Panzer Artillerie Regiment 93 (three battalions)
Heeres Flak Abteilung 304
Panzerjaeger Abteilung 93
Nachrichten Abteilung 93
Panzer Pioniere Bataillon 93

Plus divisional HQ, divisional HQ Abteilung, and divisional services.

27th Panzer Division

Began to form in France in 1942, but was sent to Russia, south, in September before its formation was complete. The division was destroyed early in 1943 and was not re-formed.

116th Panzer Division

Formed in April 1944 by the conversion of the 16th Panzergrenadier Division. The division fought in Normandy from June 1944 until the withdrawal from France at the end of August. It was moved to Düsseldorf in September for re-fitting and was then transferred to the Köln sector in November. In December it fought in the southern sector of the Ardennes offensive, where it suffered heavy losses.

In January 1945 the division was moved to the Kleve sector on the Rhine. In April it was surrounded by the Americans in the "Ruhr Pocket", where it surrendered.

Its final full establishment was:

Panzer Aufklärung Abteilung 116
Panzer Regiment 16 (two battalions)
Panzergrenadier Regiment 60 (two battalions)
Panzergrenadier Regiment 156 (two battalions)
Panzer Artillerie Regiment 146 (three battalions)
Heeres Flak Abteilung 281
Panzerjaeger Abteilung 228
Nachrichten Abteilung 228
Panzer Pioniere Bataillon 675

Plus divisional HQ, divisional HQ Abteilung, and divisional services.

Panzer Lehr Division[2]

Formed in November 1943 from the demonstration units of various training schools. Concentrated in eastern France in February 1944, the embryonic division was then transferred to Budapest in April. Here it incorporated Infanterie Lehr Regiment 901 which had been operating in the Balkans. In May the division returned to France—to the Orleans area.

When the Allied invasion of Normandy began in June 1944, the division was one of the main obstacles to the Anglo-American break-out from the bridgehead. It took a leading part in the Normandy battle and suffered heavily in the process.

After the withdrawal from France the division was sent to the Saar, and from there to Paderborn. After re-fitting as part of Sixth SS Panzer Army it returned to the Saar in November, was moved to the Eifel in December, and took part in the Ardennes offensive. It was eventually trapped in the "Ruhr Pocket" and surrendered to the Americans in April 1945.

Its final full establishment was:

Panzer Aufklärung Abteilung 130
Panzer Regiment 130 (two battalions)
Panzergrenadier Regiment 901 (two battalions)
Panzergrenadier Regiment 902 (two battalions)
Panzer Artillerie Regiment 146 (three battalions)
Heeres Flak Abteilung 311
Panzerjaeger Abteilung 130
Nachrichten Abteilung 130
Panzer Pioniere Bataillon 130

Plus divisional HQ, divisional HQ Abteilung, and divisional services.

---

[1] Like the Allies, the Germans discovered that armoured divisions in Italy, because of the nature of the terrain and the fighting, needed extra infantry. (See Duncan Crow, *British and Commonwealth Armoured Formations (1919–1946)*, Profile Publications Ltd., 1971, page 36).

[2] One authority says that the division was sometimes referred to as 130th Panzer Lehr Division. The compiler, who came across the division frequently in the North-West Europe campaign, did not, however, meet with this designation.

King Tigers (Tiger B) in a French wood during the Battle of Normandy.

Panzer Division "Gross Deutschland"

Formed as Panzer Grenadier Division "Gross Deutschland" in May 1942 from the crack motorised Infanterie Regiment "Gross Deutschland" which had fought in Poland, September 1939, and in the campaign against France, May-June 1940. "Gross Deutschland" took part in the Russian campaign from the outset, fighting in the central sector until June 1942 when it was moved to the south for three months before returning to the centre. In November 1942 it went to the south again when the Russian winter offensive began, and in February and March 1943 it was engaged in the re-capture of Kharkov and Belgorod. At the beginning of the Battle of Kursk in July 1943 "Gross Deutschland" was in 48 Panzer Corps, Fourth Panzer Army—the southern pincer. It was then transferred to the centre when the Russians began their offensive in the Orel sector later that month; after a short period it returned to 48 Panzer Corps in the south.

During the winter of 1943–44 "Gross Deutschland" was heavily engaged in the withdrawal to the Dnepr bend. In May 1944 it was moved to Bessarabia as the Russian attack reached the Dniestr and Rumania. In July it moved once again to the centre as the Russians pushed into Poland, and the following month it moved further north to Latvia and Lithuania to help in the defence of East Prussia. It fell back to Memel where it fought a rearguard action until the end of November. In December, survivors who had escaped from Memel re-formed west of Koenigsberg in East Prussia and from then until the end of March when they were overrun they fought the Russians at the Frisches Haff, the long bay at the south-east of the Gulf of Danzig.

"Gross Deutschland" was the Wehrmacht's most favoured Panzer Division. Its establishment was larger than that of an ordinary Panzer Division, larger even than that of the SS Panzer Divisions, which themselves were more favoured than the Wehrmacht divisions. Its units in 1944 were:

- Panzer Aufklärung Abteilung "Gross Deutschland"
- Panzer Regiment "Gross Deutschland" (three battalions)
- Panzer Grenadier Regiment "Gross Deutschland" (three battalions)
- Panzer Füsiliere Regiment "Gross Deutschland" (three battalions)
- Panzer Artillerie Regiment "Gross Deutschland" (three battalions)
- Heeres Flak Abteilung "Gross Deutschland"
- Panzerjaeger Abteilung "Gross Deutschland"
- Panzer Sturmgeschütz Brigade "Gross Deutschland"
- Panzer Nachrichten Abteilung "Gross Deutschland"
- Panzer Pioniere Bataillon "Gross Deutschland"

Plus divisional HQ, divisional HQ Abteilung, and divisional services. Not only did "Gross Deutschland" have a larger establishment than an ordinary Panzer Division but its actual strength kept closer to this than did the actual strengths of the run-of-the-mill Panzer Divisions which became more and more attenuated, especially in the number of tanks they had, as the war entered its later stages.

In January 1945 "Gross Deutschland" was put in control of the "Gross Deutschland Verbände" which consisted of most of the Wehrmacht's crack troops including Panzer Grenadier Division "Brandenburg", Führer Grenadier Division, Führer Begleit Division, and Panzer Division "Kurmark".

Both the Führer Begleit (Escort) and the Führer Grenadier Divisions were upgraded to divisional status from brigades in January 1945. The Führer Begleit Brigade (originally Battalion) was a motorised escort for Hitler's GHQ. To gain experience part of it saw action in Russia, north, on two occasions, but for most of the war until the end of November 1944 it was at the Führer's GHQ. In November 1944, less elements retained on guard duty, it was sent to the west to take part in the Ardennes offensive. In February, after it had been upgraded to a division, it was sent with the Führer Grenadier Division to the Oder front south-east of Berlin. It was surrounded at Spremberg near Cottbus and was virtually annihilated when breaking out on April 21, 1945. The division had a Panzer Regiment with two battalions, a Panzer Grenadier Regiment, an Infantry Battalion "for special use", an artillery Abteilung, and a Flak regiment.

The Führer Grenadier Brigade was formed as a special bodyguard after the attempt on Hitler's life on July 20, 1944. After seeing action against the Russian breakthrough at Gumbinnen in East Prussia from October to December 1944 it was sent west to take part in the Ardennes offensive. In February, now with divisional status, it was sent to Stargard east of Stettin and took part in the defence of Pomerania. At the beginning of April after fighting at Kustrin east of Berlin it was transferred to Vienna and ended the war in Austria. The division had a Panzer Regiment, a Panzer Grenadier Regiment, a motorised Panzer Grenadier Battalion, a Panzer Fusilier Battalion, an Infantry Battalion "for special use", a Panzer Sturmgeschütz Brigade, a Panzer Artillery Regiment, and a Flak Abteilung.

Panzer Division "Kurmark"

Formed in January 1945 at Cottbus south of Berlin from Kampfgruppe Langkeit its organisation was:

- Panzer Aufklärung Abteilung "Kurmark"
- Panzer Regiment "Kurmark" (two battalions)
- Panzer Grenadier Regiment "Kurmark" (two battalions)
- Panzer Artillerie Regiment "Kurmark" (two battalions)
- Panzer Nachrichten Abteilung "Kurmark"
- Panzer Pioniere Bataillon "Kurmark"

Plus divisional HQ, divisional HQ Abteilung, and divisional services.

The new division first went into action on the Oder front at the beginning of February. It remained on that front until the end of April when it broke out of Russian encirclement at Halbe, between Berlin and Cottbus, and crossed the Elbe to surrender to the Americans.

In the last stages of the war a number of scratch Panzer Divisions were formed, or were in the process of being formed when the war ended. Apart from Panzer Divisions "Kurmark" and "Feldherrnhalle 2" already mentioned, these included Panzer Divisions "Clausewitz", "Donau", "Schlesien", "Thüringen", and "Westfalen" formed in 1945 from instruction schools, training units, and reserve formations; "Kurland" formed from elements of 14th Panzer Division and motorised units in the area; "Holstein" formed from the 233rd Reserve Panzer Division; and "Münchenburg" formed from SS units.

One Panzer Division was a Luftwaffe formation, although it came under Army control after General Guderian became Inspector-General Armoured Forces in February 1943. This was

Fallschirm Panzer Division "Hermann Goering"

The "Hermann Goering" Panzer Division, composed entirely of volunteers, had its origins in the elite pre-war Luftwaffe Jaeger Regiment "Hermann Goering". In 1942 this became the "Hermann Goering" Brigade whose role was the training of paratroopers and air landing units. Early in 1943 it became first a Panzer Grenadier Division and then a Panzer Division. It was equipped in Belgium, then moved to southern France, and from there was sent to Tunisia where it was destroyed in the North African campaign which ended in May 1943.

The division was quickly re-formed in southern Italy and Sicily and played a prominent part in the Sicilian campaign in July and August 1943. It was withdrawn to Italy and in January 1944 was given the title Fallschirm Panzer Division "Hermann Goering", although the Fallschirm (Parachute) designation was purely honorary. The division became heavily engaged in containing the Anzio bridgehead from January onwards until the Allied break-out. In July it was transferred to Russia, centre, to help in trying to counter the Russian summer offensive. In August it fought at Warsaw and then in October withdrew north to East Prussia. Here it provided the cadre for Fallschirm Panzer Corps "Hermann Goering" consisting of a Panzer Division and a Panzer Grenadier Division. The Corps was engaged at Elbing, near Danzig, and broke out of Russian encirclement with heavy losses.

The establishment of Fallschirm Panzer Division "Hermann Goering" was:

- Panzer Aufklärung Abteilung "Hermann Goering"
- Panzer Regiment "Hermann Goering" (three battalions)
- Panzer Grenadier Regiment "Hermann Goering" 1 (two battalions)
- Panzer Grenadier Regiment "Hermann Goering" 2 (two battalions)[1]
- Panzer Artillerie Regiment "Hermann Goering" (four battalions)
- Flak Regiment "Hermann Goering"
- Panzer Nachrichten Abteilung "Hermann Goering"
- Panzer Pioniere Bataillon "Hermann Goering"
- Ersatz Bataillon "Hermann Goering"

[1] In each Panzer Grenadier Regiment the first battalion had three Panzer Grenadier companies, a heavy Panzer Grenadier company, and a light anti-tank company; the second battalion had three Panzer Grenadier companies, a heavy Panzer Grenadier company, a heavy anti-tank company, and two light infantry howitzer companies. The thirteenth company in the regiment was an infantry howitzer company, and the fourteenth was an anti-tank company.

Panthers (Ausf.A) of the "Gross Deutschland" Division counter-attacking near Memel, November 1944.

There were seven Panzer Divisions in the Waffen-SS. Three were formed in 1942 as Panzer Grenadier Divisions, the other four in 1943. In October 1943 all seven became Panzer Divisions.

1st SS Panzer Division "Leibstandarte SS Adolf Hitler"
Hitler's bodyguard regiment, SS Leibstandarte Adolf Hitler, was officially constituted and given its title on the National Socialist Party Day in 1933. The L.A.H. fought in Poland, September 1939, and in Flanders-France, May-June 1940. In July 1942 in France it was formed into SS Panzer Grenadier Division "Leibstandarte Adolf Hitler" with Infanterie Regiments L.A.H. 1 and 2 (from December 1942 re-designated Panzer Grenadier Regiments L.A.H. 1 and 2) each with three battalions, Panzer Regiment L.A.H. with two battalions, Aufklärung Abteilung L.A.H., Artillerie Regiment L.A.H. (three battalions), Flak Abteilung L.A.H. (five batteries), Sturmgeschütz Abteilung L.A.H. (three batteries), Panzerjaeger Abteilung L.A.H. (three companies), Nachrichten Abteilung L.A.H., Pioniere Bataillon L.A.H., and Versorgungs Einheiten L.A.H.

On October 22, 1943 the division became 1st SS Panzer Division "Leibstandarte SS Adolf Hitler". Its establishment was:

SS Panzer Aufklärung Abteilung 1
SS Panzer Regiment 1 (two battalions)
SS Panzer Grenadier Regiment 1 L.A.H. (three battalions)
SS Panzer Grenadier Regiment 2 L.A.H. (three battalions)
SS Panzer Artillerie Regiment 1 (four battalions)
SS Flak Abteilung 1 (five batteries)
SS Sturmgeschütz Abteilung 1 (three batteries)
SS Panzerjaeger Abteilung 1 (three companies)
SS Panzer Nachrichten Abteilung 1
SS Panzer Pioniere Bataillon 1
SS Versorgungs Einheiten 1
SS Werfer Abteilung 1 (from September 1944)
SS Feldersatz Bataillon 1 (from October 1944)

Plus divisional HQ, divisional HQ Abteilung, and divisional services other than the Versorgungs Einheiten.

From its formation as SS Panzer Grenadier Division L.A.H. in July 1942 until February 1943 the division remained in Normandy. It then went to Russia, south, and was part of the southern pincer in the Battle of Kursk at Belgorod in July 1943. In August it was transferred to northern Italy where it remained until the end of October when it returned to Russia, south, and fought at Zhitomir in the Ukraine and at Vinnitsa and Tscherkassy. In April 1944 it was at Tarnopol in the western Ukraine and the following month it was sent to Belgium where it was re-fitted.

In June 1944 the division joined the Normandy battle, where it fought chiefly in the Caen sector. After the withdrawal from France it fell back to the Eifel, was re-fitted in Westphalia in November, and returned to the Eifel. The division fought in the Ardennes offensive and for this operation it was allotted the 150th Panzer Brigade. In February 1945 it was moved to Hungary and ended the war in Austria.

2nd SS Panzer Division "Das Reich"
At the outbreak of the war in September 1939 the SS-Verfügungstruppen consisted of three infantry regiments, each of three battalions. These were: Standarte 1 "Deutschland", Standarte 2 "Germania", and Standarte 3 "Der Führer". The three Standarten were formed into the SS-VT Division in April 1940, and later that year, without "Germania" (see 5th SS Panzer Division "Wiking") this designation was changed to SS Division Reich and then to SS Division "Das Reich". The division was motorised.

In November 1942 the reorganised and re-equipped SS Division (Motorised) "Das Reich" which had been fighting in Russia, centre, was designated SS Panzer Grenadier Division "Das Reich" (2nd SS Division). This reorganisation took place in Normandy to which the division had been sent from Russia in June. It returned to Russia early in 1943 and fought at Kharkov, Belgorod, the Dnepr bend, Zhitomir, and Vinnitsa, before returning once again to France in April 1944, this time to the Toulouse area. By now it had been re-designated, on October 22, 1943, as 2nd SS Panzer Division "Das Reich".

The division was moved up to Normandy after the Allied landings. It went into action against First U.S. Army early in July 1944. After the defeat in France the division withdrew to the Eifel area and then, after being re-equipped, took part in the Ardennes offensive. With the rest of Sixth SS Panzer Army it was moved east to Hungary in January 1945 and ended the war near Linz, where it surrendered to the Americans.

The division's establishment was:

Aufklärung Abteilung SS Panzer Division "Das Reich"
Panzer Regiment 2 SS Panzer Division "Das Reich" (two battalions)
SS Panzer Grenadier Regiment 3 "Deutschland" (three battalions)
SS Panzer Grenadier Regiment 4 "Der Führer" (three battalions)
Artillerie Regiment SS Panzer Division "Das Reich" (four battalions)
Flak Abteilung SS Panzer Division "Das Reich"
Sturmgeschutz Abteilung SS Panzer Division "Das Reich"
Panzer Jaeger Abteilung SS Panzer Division "Das Reich"
Nachrichten Abteilung SS Panzer Division "Das Reich"
Pioniere Bataillon SS Panzer Division "Das Reich"

Plus divisional HQ, divisional HQ Abteilung, and divisional services. In 1943 Panzer Grenadier Regiment SS "Langemark" (two battalions) was attached to the division.

3rd SS Panzer Division "Totenkopf"
In October 1939 after the Polish campaign the first three SS "Totenkopf" regiments were formed into the SS Division Totenkopf (motorised). In November 1942 in southern France, after serving in Russia, this became the SS Panzer Grenadier Division "Totenkopf" and then on October 22, 1943 it was re-designated 3rd SS Panzer Division "Totenkopf". By this time the division was in the Dnepr bend, having returned to Russia, south, in February 1943, to fight at Kharkov in March and Belgorod in the Battle of Kursk in July. It remained on the Eastern front until the end of the war, fighting in the southern Ukraine until July 1944 when it was moved to Bialystok, north-east of Warsaw. In January 1945 it

was transferred from the Eastern front, centre, to Hungary, and from there fell back through Vienna to Linz where it surrendered to the Americans in May 1945.

The division's establishment was:

- Aufklärung Abteilung SS Panzer Division "Totenkopf"
- Panzer Regiment 3 SS Panzer Division "Totenkopf" (two battalions)
- SS Panzer Grenadier Regiment 5 "Thule" (three battalions)
- SS Panzer Grenadier Regiment 6 "Theodor Eicke" (three battalions)
- Artillerie Regiment SS Panzer Division "Totenkopf" (four battalions)
- Flak Abteilung SS Panzer Division "Totenkopf"
- Sturmgeschütz Abteilung SS Panzer Division "Totenkopf"
- Panzer Jaeger Abteilung SS Panzer Division "Totenkopf"
- Nachrichten Abteilung SS Panzer Division "Totenkopf"
- Pioniere Bataillon SS Panzer Division "Totenkopf"

Plus divisional HQ, divisional HQ Abteilung, and divisional services. In 1942, when it was the SS Division "Totenkopf", "Freikorps Danmark" served in the division.

5th SS Panzer Division "Wiking"

Late in 1940 SS Regiment "Germania" together with SS Regiment "Nordland" (raised from Danish and Norwegian Nazi sympathisers), SS Regiment "Westland" (raised from the Netherlands and Belgium), and the 5th SS Artillery Regiment, formed the "Germania" SS Division. Soon afterwards this title was changed to "Wiking" SS Division. The division fought in Russia.

In November 1942 in the Caucasus the division was re-formed into SS Panzer Grenadier Division "Wiking". It fought on the Manych with Fourth Panzer Army at the beginning of 1943 and then with First Panzer Army in the Kharkov area from February to August, falling back to the Dnepr bend. On October 22, 1943 it was re-designated 5th SS Panzer Division "Wiking".

From January to March 1944 the division continued to fight in Russia, south. It was then moved to Russia, centre, to Kovel east of Lublin. From May to July it was back in Germany, re-fitting at Heidelager, and then returned to the Eastern front, centre. In January 1945 it was moved south to Hungary and it ended the war at Graz, Austria.

The division's establishment was:

- Aufklärung Abteilung 5 SS Panzer Division "Wiking"
- SS Panzer Abteilung "Wiking" (two battalions)
- SS Panzer Grenadier Regiment 9 "Germania" (three battalions)
- SS Panzer Grenadier Regiment 10 "Westland" (three battalions)
- Artillerie Regiment 5 SS Panzer Division "Wiking" (four battalions)
- Flak Abteilung 5 SS Panzer Division "Wiking"
- Panzer Jaeger Abteilung 5 SS Panzer Division "Wiking"
- Nachrichten Abteilung 5 SS Panzer Division "Wiking"
- Pioniere Bataillon 5 SS Panzer Division "Wiking"
- Feldersatz Bataillon 5 SS Panzer Division "Wiking"
- Versorgungs Einheiten

Plus divisional HQ, divisional HQ Abteilung, and divisional services other than the Versorgungs Einheiten.

9th SS Panzer Division "Hohenstaufen"

Formed in the winter 1942–43 in Berlin as the 9th SS Panzer Grenadier Division it was sent to Ypres in Belgium to complete its formation. On October 22, 1943 the division was re-designated 9th SS Panzer Division "Hohenstaufen".

Its establishment was:

- SS Panzer Aufklärung Abteilung 9
- SS Panzer Regiment 9 (two battalions)
- SS Panzer Grenadier Regiment 19 (three battalions)
- SS Panzer Grenadier Regiment 20 (three battalions)
- SS Panzer Artillerie Regiment 9 (four battalions)
- SS Flak Abteilung 9
- SS Sturmgeschütz Abteilung 9
- SS Panzer Jaeger Abteilung 9
- SS Nachrichten Abteilung 9
- SS Pioniere Bataillon 9

Plus divisional HQ, divisional HQ Abteilung, and divisional services.

The division was formed at the same time as the 10th SS Panzer Division "Frundsberg" and with it formed II SS Panzer Corps. In March 1944 it was moved from Ypres to southern France and from there, almost immediately, with 10th SS Panzer Division to the Ukraine to meet a crisis that had developed there. It fought in the Tarnopol sector and then in June was abruptly ordered west, again with 10th SS Panzer Division, to take part in the Normandy battle. II SS Panzer Corps came into action in Normandy during the afternoon of June 29.

After the Normandy defeat the division was re-fitted in the Netherlands and was at Arnhem when the Allied airborne landings took place. It played a major part in defeating that operation. It then took part in the Ardennes offensive as part of Sixth SS Panzer Army, was moved to Hungary in February still as part of that army with the 1st, 2nd and 12th SS Panzer Divisions, and ended the war in Austria.

10th SS Panzer Division "Frundsberg"

Formed in the winter 1942–43 in the south of France as the 10th SS Panzer Grenadier Division. In June 1943 its designation was changed to 10th SS Division "Karl der Grosse", and then, on October 3, on Hitler's order, to SS Panzer Division Frundsberg. Finally, on October 22, it was re-designated 10th SS Panzer Division "Frundsberg". Its two Panzer Grenadier Regiments were changed from 1 and 2 (Frundsberg) to SS Panzer Grenadier Regiments 21 and 22, each with three battalions. The rest of the division's establishment was SS Kradschützen Regiment 10 (two battalions), SS Panzer Regiment 10 "Langemark" (two battalions), SS Panzer Artillerie Regiment 10 (four battalions), SS Flak Abteilung 10, SS Sturmgeschütz Abteilung 10 SS Panzer Jaeger Abteilung 10, SS Nachrichten Abteilung 10, SS Pioniere Bataillon 10, and divisional HQ, divisional HQ Abteilung, and divisional services.

After the completion of its formation the division

moved to northern France in November 1943. It stayed there until March 1944, when it was moved with 9th SS Panzer Division to the Ukraine. It fought at Tarnopol and Lvov and was then ordered to France on June 12, with 9th SS Panzer Division, to join in the Normandy battle. It came into action on June 29 against the British 8 Corps bridgehead across the River Odon.

The division was re-fitted in the Netherlands and was in the Arnhem area when the Allied Operation "Market Garden" took place on September 17; it was sent to defend Nijmegen. In December it took part in the Ardennes offensive, was subsequently moved to Pomerania, and after hard fighting there, on the Oder, and in Lausitz, it surrendered to the Russians in Saxony at the end of the war.

12th SS Panzer Division "Hitlerjugend"

Formed as a Panzer Grenadier Division on July 20, 1943 at Antwerp from cadres of Leibstandarte Adolf Hitler and personnel of the Hitlerjugend Leadership schools. The division was to form I SS Panzer Corps with Leibstandarte Adolf Hitler. On October 21 Hitler ordered that the Corps was to consist of two Panzer Divisions; consequently, the following day, the division was re-designated 12th SS Panzer Division "Hitlerjugend". Its two Panzer Grenadier Regiments had their designations changed from 1 and 2 (Hitlerjugend) to SS Panzer Grenadier Regiments 25 and 26, each with three battalions. The rest of the division's establishment was SS Panzer Aufklärung Abteilung 12, SS Panzer Regiment 12 (two battalions), SS Panzer Artillerie Regiment 12 (three battalions), SS Panzer Flak Abteilung 12, SS Werfer Abteilung 12, SS Panzer Jaeger Abteilung 12, SS Panzer Nachrichten Abteilung 12, SS Panzer Pioniere Bataillon 12, and divisional HQ, divisional HQ Abteilung, and divisional services.

The division first went into action on June 7, 1944 in the Caen area in Normandy. It provided the backbone to the defence against First Canadian Army during the Battle of Falaise, and then fell back to the Eifel. It was re-fitted at Bremen, took part in the Ardennes offensive, and was then moved to Hungary as part of Sixth SS Panzer Army with three other SS Panzer Divisions—1st, 2nd and 9th—a move which began on January 20, 1945. At the end of the war the division was in Austria where it surrendered with the rest of what was left of Sixth SS Panzer Army.

GLOSSARY

Abteilung—Company, Detachment
Artillerie—Artillery
Aufklärung—Reconnaissance
Bataillon—Battalion
Flak (Flugabwehrkanone)—Anti-Aircraft Gun
Heeres—Army
Nachrichten—Signals
Panzer—Armour(ed), Tank
Panzerjaeger—Tank Destroyer (lit. Hunter)
Pioniere—Engineers
Sturmgeschütz—Assault Gun
Werfer—(Rocket) projector

Field-Marshal Rudolf Gerd von Rundstedt, Commander-in-Chief West. He had previously commanded Army Group South against Poland in 1939, Army Group A (which had the decisive role) against France in 1940, and Army Group South against Russia in 1941–42.

Tiger B, or King Tiger, with turret traversed to seven o'clock, knocked out in Normandy.

PANZER DIVISION

		Officers	Other Ranks	Rifles or Carbines	Pistols	Sub-MGs	LMGs	Heavy MGs	81-mm Mortars	120-mm Mortars	Flame Throwers	20-mm Anti-Aircraft Guns	20-mm Anti-Tank Guns	28/20-mm Anti-Tank Guns	37-mm Anti-Aircraft Guns (Self-Propelled)	75-mm Anti-Tank Guns (Towed)	75-mm Anti-Tank Guns (Self-Propelled)	75-mm Tank Guns (L/43 or L/48)	75-mm Tank Guns (L/70)	88-mm Anti-Aircraft Guns	75-mm Infantry Howitzers (Self-Propelled)	150-mm Infantry Howitzers (Self-Propelled)	105-mm Gun Howitzers (Towed)	105-mm Howitzers (Self-Propelled)	150-mm Howitzers (Towed)	150-mm Howitzers (Self-Propelled)	PzKpfw IV	PzKpfw V Panther	Motor Vehicles	Motor-cycles	
(a)	Div. H.Q.	32	109	95	44	3																							32	8	(a)
(b)	Div. H.Q. Abteilung	3	216	138	65	19	16	2	2			4					3												31	28	(b)
(c)	Panzer Aufklärung Abteilung	27	915	434	300	206	147	4	10		6		35				13												199	22	(c)
(d)	Panzer Regiment	69	1,592	822	704	228	252					6			8			52	51								52	51	313	53	(d)
(e)	Panzer Grenadier Regiment[1]	64	2,230	1,373	595	336	224	24	14	8	24	25									12	6							406	81	(e)
(f)	Panzer Grenadier Regiment[2]	61	2,197	1,449	574	235	144	26	14	8	18	12										6							380	83	(f)
(g)	Artillery Regiment	69	1,580	1,217	343	203	92					9											12	12	12	6			407	31	(g)
(h)	Heeres Flak Abteilung	22	742	673	69	47	18					18								8									171	16	(h)
(i)	Panzerjaeger Abteilung	20	493	271	142	100	47									12	31												135	17	(i)
(j)	Nachrichten Abteilung	16	499	444	69	51	35																						114	14	(j)
(k)	Panzer Pioniere Bataillon	24	861	562	247	102	96	6	6		20		3	3															174	42	(k)
(l)	Div. Services	64	1,821	1,708	165	13	86																						323	85	(l)
		471	13,255	9,186	3,317	1,543	1,157	64	46	16	68	74	38	3	8	12	47	52	51	8	12	12	12	12	12	6	52	51	2,685*	480	

13,726 (Officers and Other Ranks)

[1] Armoured.
[2] Motorised

*including 357 armoured vehicles

SS PANZER DIVISION

		Officers	Other Ranks	Rifles or Carbines	Pistols	Sub-MGs	LMGs	Heavy MGs	81-mm Mortars	120-mm Mortars	Flame Throwers	150- or 210-mm Rocket Projectors	20-mm Anti-Aircraft Guns	20-mm Anti-Tank Guns	28/20-mm Anti-Tank Guns	37-mm Anti-Aircraft Guns (Self-Propelled)	75-mm Anti-Tank Guns (Towed)	75-mm Anti-Tank Guns (Self-Propelled)	75-mm Tank Guns (L/43 or L/48)	75-mm Tank Guns (L/70)	88-mm Anti-Aircraft Guns	75-mm Infantry Howitzers (Self-Propelled)	150-mm Infantry Howitzers (Self-Propelled)	105-mm Gun Howitzers (Towed)	105-mm Gun Howitzers (Self-Propelled)	150-mm Howitzers (Towed)	150-mm Howitzers (Self-Propelled)	170-mm Guns	PzKpfw IV	PzKpfw V Panther	Motor Vehicles	Motor-cycles	
(a)	Div. H.Q.	32	109	95	44	3																									32	8	(a)
(b)	Div. H.Q. Abteilung	3	216	138	65	19	16	2	2				4					3													31	28	(b)
(c)	Panzer Aufklärung Abteilung	27	915	434	300	206	147	4	10		6			35				13													193	22	(c)
(d)	Panzer Regiment	70	1,701	816	719	245	296						6			8			64	62									64	62	313	53	(d)
(e)	Panzer Grenadier Regiment	89	3,153	1,957	852	443	284	38	20	12	24		43									12	6								527	88	(e)
(f)	Panzer Grenadier Regiment	89	3,153	1,957	852	443	284	38	20	12	24		43									12	6								527	88	(f)
(g)	Panzer Artillerie Regiment	89	2,078	1,636	409	255	109	12																12	12	12	6	12			534	40	(g)
(h)	Flak Abteilung	22	802	729	73	47	22						18								12										181	16	(h)
(i)	Sturmgeschütz Abteilung	15	329	294	80	70	22											22													100	11	(i)
(j)	Panzerjaeger Abteilung	20	493	271	142	100	47										12	31													135	17	(j)
(k)	Panzer Nachrichten Abteilung	16	499	444	69	51	35																								114	14	(k)
(l)	Panzer Pioniere Bataillon	26	958	654	254	102	99	6	6		20			3	3																212	52	(l)
(m)	Werfer Abteilung	14	459	380	40	53	18					18																			107	8	(m)
(n)	Div. Services	64	1,821	1,708	165	13	86																								323	85	(n)
		576	16,868	11,513	4,064	2,050	1,465	100	58	24	74	18	114	38	3	8	12	69	64	62	12	24	12	12	12	12	6	12	64	62	3,329*	530	

17,262 (Officers and Other Ranks)

*including 359 armoured vehicles

Index